Cumberland
Museum & Archives

A Place Called CUMBERLAND

Edited by
Rhonda Bailey

Figure.1
Vancouver/Toronto/Berkeley

24 25 26 27 28   5 4 3 2 1

Cataloguing data is available from Library and Archives Canada
ISBN 978-1-77327-251-1 (pbk.)

Design by Teresa Bubela

Editing by Michael Leyne and Mélanie Ritchot
Copy editing by Lesley Cameron
Proofreading by Tanya Trafford
Indexing by Stephen Ullstrom

Cover artwork by Jennifer Eaton
Map courtesy of Cumberland Museum & Archives Collection, 990.057.005
Back cover photograph courtesy of Daryl Calnan
Front flap photograph courtesy of Jim Whyte

Printed and bound in China by Shenzhen Reliance Printing Co., Ltd.

Figure 1 Publishing Inc.
Vancouver BC Canada
www.figure1publishing.com

Figure 1 Publishing is located in the traditional, unceded territory of the xʷməθkʷəy̓əm (Musqueam), Sḵwx̱wú7mesh (Squamish), and səlilwətaɬ (Tsleil-Waututh) peoples.

We are grateful for the generous financial support provided by the Y.P. Heung Foundation.

But it takes more than bricks, mortar or lumber to make a city. It takes people. The people of Cumberland, coming from diverse backgrounds and bound by the common bond of their work with its inherent hazards, were unique in many ways. Their sturdy independence was forged through adversity, strikes and disasters, and their fierce loyalty to their city and parochial pride in its institutions were sometimes a source of wonder to the stranger.

BILL JOHNSTONE, *COAL DUST IN MY BLOOD*, 2002.

Contents

Preface

This book is a collection of narratives by a talented group of authors who are all connected by their relationships to a geographic place: the place now known as Cumberland.

People are drawn to places for many reasons—opportunities, resources, or an attraction to the natural landscape—but it is the many human connections that bring individuals together, create lasting memories, cultivate our sense of self, and build our ideals about community.

My connection to Cumberland started in March 2020—just before COVID-19 was officially declared to be a pandemic—when I became the director of the Cumberland Museum & Archives. The shuttered and seemingly abandoned downtown was an echo of its former vibrant self; people wandered through the Community Forest, drawing solace and strength from the lush wooded sanctuary during an uncertain time, not unlike those who escaped to Comox Lake during the Big Strike of 1912–1913 or the Spanish influenza pandemic. Over the following year, I witnessed first-hand a community in hibernation slowly come back to life. As time passed and COVID restrictions were lifted, the community rallied to support businesses by eating and shopping locally. The lines outside of Riders Pizza and the Cumberland Brewing

Company became meeting places for neighbours as life returned to a more regular routine.

At the Cumberland Museum & Archives, we delved into our own form of escapism: a large-scale renovation project. On October 1, 2020, we intentionally closed our doors. Staff and volunteers carefully emptied the exhibitions and collections space of artefacts, furniture, and fixtures. We devoted ourselves to examining the fundamental concept of what the museum meant to the community and to looking at how the museum disseminates the many diverse and divergent perspectives that shape human histories.

To me, a museum is a home filled with belongings for safekeeping, a place of memory-building and community-gathering. Like every community, every organization has been touched by those who have played a role in its past. Dedication and care were evident in every collections box, in words written on didactic panels, and even in the concrete path in the old mine structure. We saw our reimagining of the museum not as a blank canvas on which to start anew but as an opportunity to build on the work of our predecessors and continue to share the storied histories of our community.

The *Glasgow Museum Display Guideline: A Practical Guide for Exhibitions* has a rule: no more than one hundred words per panel. This rule helped our team create concise and informative narratives to draw in visitors and guide them through our physical spaces. However, as we leafed through archival documents and researched the stories of community members, events, and the evolving and complex needs of the people of Cumberland, it became clear that one hundred words were not nearly enough. Thus, the idea for this publication was born: a collection of narratives that centre on shared human experiences and relationships that create our sense of place here in Cumberland.

A Place Called Cumberland brings together established authors and authors whose work is being published for the first time. Gathering a group of potential contributors, each with their own area of interests and expertise, was a unique coming-together process. Once the project work started, a small working group was formed: Lynne Bowen, a celebrated historian and Vancouver Island author; Cumberland's own Kim Bannerman, a passionate, seasoned storyteller in the realms of fiction and nonfiction alike; and last but not least, Dawn Copeman, a museum colleague, friend, and amazing steward of community history. These three women met on Zoom calls and worked with me to articulate the swirl of ideas and concepts I had for the book and formulated them into a framework we could use to approach others and invite them to join our literary journey. Each working group member recommended between one and three contributors for the project.

It was important to our working committee that this book reflect not only the well-known stories and histories of Cumberland but the lesser-known ones too. A key component of the book's composition was that each narrative be rooted in primary resources and research yet accessible to a contemporary audience through a creative nonfiction style. Each contributing author has their own voice and their own descriptive tone, a reflection of their own process and prose—just like the many individuals of Cumberland.

The challenge that followed was how to make sense of the multitude of voices and draft a manuscript that flowed. Luckily, Rhonda Bailey, a retired professional editor and long-time colleague of Lynne's, joined us as the project's developmental editor. Rhonda was brilliant, bringing our beautifully crafted chaos into order and working with each individual contributor to ensure everyone held true to the intentions of the project yet maintained their individuality.

As the drafts came in, I found myself lost in the unfurling history of each contributor's reflections, in a complex interplay of connections. The book opens with an introduction to Cumberland through the eyes of a newcomer in the cold, damp winter. Looking through a window into her experience of isolation had me contemplating how it takes time to root ourselves in new places and new experiences. From this opening story, we take a step back in time with stories of grit, adventure, mystery, resistance, and resilience born from an influx of settlement driven by resource extraction. We then move into a more contemporary age, with a ride in the forest, a walk down Dunsmuir Avenue, and a reflection on the raw relationships and challenges of our current community.

A Place Called Cumberland is a journey through personal accounts, dialogues, and a palimpsest of memories layered with care and compassion, all representing different experiences and times of discovery. Some stories will have you on the edge of your seat; others will have you noticing a tear in your eye, or making you feel inspired by the strength of individuals and the collective community.

The impressions of human experience we leave in our wake are touchstones for the next generation. The start of a journey of discovery. We hope you find an experience that resonates, an unknown fact, a sense of belonging as you, the reader, are welcomed into our community through the pages of this book.

—Rosslyn Shipp, Executive Director,
Cumberland Museum & Archives

Acknowledgements

tuwa akʷs χoχoɬ ʔa xʷ yiχmɛtɛt (ʔa) kʷʊms hɛhaw tʊms gɩǰɛ
—"Caretakers of the 'Land of Plenty' since time immemorial"

Since time immemorial, ancestors of the people called K'ómoks today, consisting of the Pentlatch, Ieeksan (pronounced "eye-ick-sun"), Sasitla ("sa-seet-la"), Xa'xe ("ha-hey"), and Sathloot ("sath-loot") peoples, have been the caretakers of this land, which they called the "Land of Plenty." This Land of Plenty stretched from what is known today as Kelsey Bay in the north down to Hornby and Denman Islands in the south, and included the watershed and estuary of the Puntledge River. For ancestors of the K'ómoks First Nation, the land now known as Cumberland was "The Way Between": a passageway for people and for trade with the Nuu-chah-nulth groups of western Vancouver Island.

The movement of people from place to place leaves a trail of interconnected impressions that carve out pathways and rest stops on each of our journeys. We acknowledge that the land on which we have come together to create this publication is the unceded traditional territory of the K'ómoks First Nation and that we are visitors on their land. The stories shared in this book are all written from a settler's viewpoint. Museums and historians in both the past and contemporary times overwhelmingly focused on European and colonial points of view, ignoring, disparaging, or erasing the stories of oppressed and marginalized groups. This book shares a selection of narratives that reflect their authors' own experiences and connection to place. There are so many more untold stories, unheard voices, and unwritten words; yet then and now, we are all connected by our ties to this land. As our journeys continue, it is crucial to foster an openness to listen, learn, and lean into acknowledging the complicated and complex relationships of people, place, and land through our collective impact on each other.

This project would not have been possible without the contributions of many, many people. I would like to thank each contributing author for lending their words, time, and talents to this project. To Lynne, Kim, Dawn, and Rhonda, thank you for your words of encouragement and for supporting my vision. The time I spent with you on emails and Zoom meetings was a treasured part of getting to know you and learning a thing or two about the literary process. Without this working group, there would not be a publication.

To Raymond, Terri, and Elsie Heung of the Y.P. Heung Foundation, thank you for your continued support for Cumberland Museum & Archives projects. It was through our initial conversations (usually over a glass of wine) that the ideas for this publication began to take shape: a book that would elevate the stories of Cumberland beyond the Comox Valley and deepen the knowledge of British Columbia's rural communities. To Catherine Clement, Eden Lindsay-Bodie, and Elizabeth Peterson, along with Raymond Heung, Elsie Heung, and Dawn Copeman, thank you for your work on the Museum's Advisory Committee not only for this project but also for several others. Your insights, experience, and knowledge helped nurture a professional dialogue that strengthened the overall vision of the publication.

Figure 1 Publishing: it has been an immense pleasure to work with each member of your team. Thank you for your expertise, guidance, and attention to detail. Your commitment to excellence in publishing and the collaborative process made the coordination of this project seamless.

To the community of Cumberland and to you the reader, thank you for joining the journey.

—Rosslyn Shipp, Executive Director,
Cumberland Museum & Archives

Circa 1999

TRACI SKUCE

It's November 1999. The millennium turns over in less than two months. Y2K is right around the corner. But it seems like you've fallen back in time. No, not back exactly. Not like that story where the girl tries on the coat in the attic and hears clomping horses outside her window. There's none of that. But it's like you're halted behind the momentum of the future. As the whole world moves forward in time—by centuries, by millennia—this village seems inert. Almost fossilized.

Because: Where are you?

This is what friends ask. The ones you left behind in Victoria. And the ones in Toronto.

At the foothills of the Beaufort Mountains, you reply. In a village—a fucking village. Not a single traffic light. Your mail goes to a box in the post office. And the library's a tiny hole in the wall. Closed half the week. It was your boyfriend's idea, moving here. After a summer working together, after travelling through

Lake Country, after hiking all over Haida Gwaii, he was heading home to Quebec. He tells this story over and over. Leaning forward, one hand on the table, the other gesticulating. Explaining how he slowed his van down as he thought of you, as he asked himself, did he really think he was going to find someone else, someone better? Why not you?

And so, he pulled into a gas station outside Chilliwack and fed quarters into a payphone and called you. You'd been staying at your dad's in Victoria, having packed your entire apartment into storage before you dragged your four-year-old son to a bush camp in the middle of the Rockies. You'd known you wanted to move. Enough of city life, you'd thought. What you'd pictured: gardens, communal living, a yoga studio with autumnal light slanting through the windows. So, when your boyfriend called, you imagined all this, plus his tall, thin body, his dark curls and the way they fell over his azure eyes. You thought of all the ways he'd touched you, *wanted* you, so that when he proposed Cumberland—a town close to a ski hill (for him) but still on the Island (for you)—you said yes without a single thought.

The day after you moved here, a fog settled over the valley, and two days after that, the clocks dropped back an hour. Ever since, your ears have been plugged.

Unpacking the kitchen stuff, your books, your son's toys.

Every movement feels like you're swimming upstream. The world muffled and rushing by.

THE BUNGALOW YOU'VE rented is freezing. Oil heat and single-paned windows, and you swear that fog seeps through every crack and right into your bones. Despite the three pairs of socks, the slippers, the sweaters, you're chilled. You drink mug after mug of tea. Whenever the heat kicks on, your son runs sockless across the bare wood floor and stands over one of the heat vents. His little nose is in a perpetual sniffle, his wide and open eyes fixed on you.

How about we go for a walk? you say.

He wipes his nose with the back of his hand. Nope, he says, and tells you about the Lego structure he's in the throes of.

What if we get donuts? you say.

He blinks twice and darts back into his room for socks.

THERE'S A DRIZZLE OUTSIDE. This persistent fog. And although it feels like four in the afternoon, it's only noon. Your son skips ahead and then dawdles behind you, an endless chatter spilling from his mouth. You don't even know what he's saying.

You pass a triangular chunk of green space. A wood-carved sign reads Peace Park. Your son asks three times what it says before you answer. He races forward again, saying Pizza Park, over and over.

Past the Peace (Pizza) Park is a shingled shack, brick red with dying vines clinging to the base. There's a plaque in front that says it's a heritage site, an artifact from the coal-mining days, housing for the newly shipped brides before (or if ever) their larger homes were ever built. Many women arriving after a days-long journey from Nanaimo, even longer from Vancouver, suitcases or steamer trunks full of inadequate clothes, full of hopeful china, some of the china now broken. All the family, friends they'd said goodbye to. The muddied roads, the gritty, coal-dusted husbands to greet them, to show them inside the small boxes they would somehow call home. Bridal Alley it was called. Meaning a row of such shacks. Each containing its own bewildered, recently married woman.

You're projecting, of course.

All through history: women uprooting their entire lives to move elsewhere for a man.

YOU'VE HEARD ABOUT the donuts from various sources. The woman from the rental agency when you signed the lease. The cashier at the Thrifty's in Courtenay when you told her you'd just moved to the Valley. The one friend you know from your university days. But when you open the bakery door and the bells tingle above, a stern-faced woman tells you you're out of luck. Gotta get here early, she says. Donuts are definitely gone before noon. Your son's face falls into a pout, and you promise to get him something else.

But what else is there?

The display case looks depleted. Only a few bags of dinner rolls, a couple loaves of that ridged malt bread, and some tarts.

No cookies? you say.

And the woman points to a small row of raisin oatmeal. You buy one for your son, promising him you'll pick out all the raisins.

AFTER THE COOKIE, you find yourself at the museum. It's as renowned as the donuts, or so you've been told, but it's tiny, twice the square footage of your bungalow. Your son rips around the upstairs exhibit, and you follow, half-exhausted, annoyed even, that the museum is so small.

You grew up in Toronto. As a kid, you spent entire Saturdays exploring dinosaur bones and Egyptian artifacts. The hour-long excursion you had in mind for the Cumberland museum shrivels to maybe fifteen minutes.

Photos along the wall show early days of colonization. Darkly dressed people with iron-like expressions. Steam donkeys. Rail cars. Mine sites in action. Passages of text beneath. But the fog has entered your head, taken up temporary residence; sentences detailing the village's history swim through your brain without making sense.

Mama! your son shouts.

He's over by what looks like an antique appliance. What's this? he says, looping around an oblong, bubble-shaped apparatus with a chalky turquoise exterior. It looks decorative. As though magnets might be stuck all over it. One of your son's drawings with the fire engines. When you step closer, you see there are little skylight windows on the top, along the sides, and you discover it's an iron lung.

An *iron lung*.

At first you imagine men lying inside it. Inert, contained, coal dust clogging the tiny branches of their lungs. But then you see it was for people who had polio. Big outbreaks in the 1940s and '50s, and those unlucky few who experienced respiratory paralysis. The iron lung an exterior diaphragm for those who could no longer breathe alone. What kind of life is that? Encased in such a contraption—maybe in a parlour or a bedroom—life going on around you.

Your son asks what this thing is for anyway. A machine to help people breathe, you say. If they got a disease, they had trouble breathing.

His small face puzzles and he says, I can do that all by myself, see? And he sucks the museum air up his two snotty nostrils until his good pink lungs become balloons.

THE MILLENNIUM WON'T matter here, you think. There's nothing really to shut down. Plus, none of the shop windows are filled with Y2K survival kits or warnings. In fact, the shops seem to open only haphazardly. The used bookshop you've passed by three times in the past week has a sign taped to the door. Call if you're interested in browsing, it says. Plus, all the second-hand places—with antiques and used furniture—seem uninterested in doing any actual business. Not that you've got much money for them. Your summer earnings are dwindling; you keep praying that this Y2K thing will eradicate your student loan. But you doubt it.

There's no work. Judging from the classifieds anyway. It used to be different, people tell you. The mines, the logging. Men moving from all over to cash in. You're pretty sure you saw a sign that said the white miners earned two bucks a day, any person of colour got a dollar. Yes, times were different. But you suspect a lot of indentured servitude went on.

And the women.

Waiting in those tiny shacks while their husbands drank their wages.

THE FOG WON'T LIFT.

Your boyfriend seems unbothered by it. He's been up the mountain all week, first aid training with the ski patrol. No fog up there, he says, pouring you another glass of wine while you teeter on your wobbly chair and poke at a plate of roasted yams. You get above it, he says.

What are we doing here? you say. I still can't figure that out.

Remember when we found this place? he says. Back in September? Remember how beautiful you said it was?

Your son is in the living room watching *Babe* for the bazillionth time. He laughs the same way every time Ferdinand the duck gives his little speech to Babe. He's laughing now.

You sip the wine. Push all the yams to the rim of the plate. Notice it's chipped. No, you say. I'm not seeing the beauty.

Fear and regret swing on the branches of your lungs. Somersault around your heart. I'm still trying to figure out why we're here, you say.

Well, your boyfriend says, corking the bottle, it *is* November.

OUT OF YOUR HOUSE and down at the end of your street is a trail that leads into forest. Your neighbour, an old-timer, says the forest used to be a field. Played baseball there, he says. And before that, the mines.

The trail leads through sizable firs and cedars, a sprinkle of hemlock, all there of their own accord. Meaning this isn't a replanted forest, a plantation like so many in this province, but a living, layered ecosystem. The ground soft under your muddied boots, the mosses glowing from within. The sheen of salal leaves. Respite from the interminable November dark, this unmitigated fog.

Your son's dashing up ahead, making motor sounds with his mouth, and you're wondering what you'll do with him all day. All week. The whole next millennium. You miss your best friend in Victoria, the days and days you spent together, letting your kids play while you bemoaned your exhaustion or laughed about the hippie men at the family dance. But you have no friends here, and your boyfriend is up the mountain; you feel a deep loneliness clinging to the insides of your throat.

If you were another kind of woman, you'd howl, scream into the muffled sky, and wail right into the next millennium. Instead, you hold it together for your son, the nearby neighbours, the trees.

Your son circles back to you when the trail forks. Which way? he says. Which way? You tell him to choose and watch his small back disappear to the left, into a corridor of alders.

You follow, and there's a clearing; no, not a clearing, but trees and brush creating a circle, an overhang over a concrete structure. For a moment, just a flash, you wish it was Baba Yaga's chicken-legged house, a place for you to retrieve a set of instructions, something to clarify why you're here and what you should be doing. But there's no Baba Yaga and no Baba Yaga's house, only, it's a three-walled graffitied room with no roof. A cold fire ring on the concrete floor, smashed glass and those ubiquitous Lucky Lager cans scattered about.

There's no commemorative sign to let you know this was a mine site. But if you busted apart the space below the fire ring, the earth would present like a wound. A wound men used to descend into, with mules and drills and picks. The dampness of it, the gases, the threat, always, of being trapped.

Imagine it.

Days closed in like that, the ache in your spine, the dim light from your helmet. One year turning into ten. Wages always shy of that better life.

You've lived above ground your whole life, have only once been inside a pitch-dark cave. You remember how thin the air felt, the way your heart crawled up your throat and pounded in such complete and absolute darkness.

YOUR BOYFRIEND FINISHES his first aid course and tells you to go off on your own, leave your son with him.

Explore, he says. We'll play Uno. He kisses the top of your head.

You're much faster without your son. A little lightness spreads through your body as you hoof across the broken pavement, over sidewalks that disappear and reappear throughout the village. No rhyme or reason, except, you imagine, paltry budgets.

Fog hangs low over the three hotel bars on Dunsmuir, the library, the Big Store, and the faux-front building beside the museum.

You keep walking. Turn the corner you will come to turn thousands of times. Onto the lake road and under a canopy of bare-branched maples and cottonwoods, all the way to a small parking lot.

You stop and approach a cabin built of timbers. Jumbo's Cabin, a sign says. No bigger than the bridal shack. It's boarded up so you can't enter. The sign says something about how Jumbo used to live there, on the edge of these swamplands, cottonwoods thick as ancient temple columns, a whole grove of alders.

This place used to be known as Chinatown. Migrant workers who came to labour in the mines, segregated and living in the swamp. Of course, there were buildings, like Jumbo's Cabin and a whole host of others, but now you walk and the land feels like a palimpsest, a text of lives lived that you can no longer read but know existed. Even though, in the '60s, the village condemned all the buildings in Chinatown, torched them to the ground.

MID-NOVEMBER AND THE DAY, though slow to dawn, offers you something you feel you've almost forgotten.

Sun.

You stand on your front porch to receive it. Gaze out over the Village, which appears, after all that fog, in sharp relief.

Wood smoke spills from your neighbour's chimney. An ATV roars down the road behind your house, and then it is silent.

Here you are.

In a place called Cumberland.

At a time that is a turning of centuries, millennia.

You close your eyes and imagine this place from long ago.

Before it was Cumberland or Union.

Before colonizers set foot here, before they razed the forests, built roads and rails, before they sniffed out seams of coal and ripped open the earth to extract it. Before they stole this land from entire nations, infected them with smallpox, before they seized their children and forced them into residential schools.

Back when the land was the land and people lived on it. Knew it. Respected it.

The November sun rises a little higher now. Floods its brothy light over the rounded peaks of the Beauforts, over the valleys and swales of forest.

Of course, you cannot turn back time. Or even sink back into it. And history is layered and complicated and never one-sided. So what are *you* doing here? Where do *you* fit in?

You have no answer. But you will come to walk this Village and the land around it. Over and over for years, for decades, you will walk across pavements and forest floors, over histories and millennia, and you will let the land rise up through your feet, inform your body, your breath. In this way you will learn to love this place. In this way, it will become home.

Your boyfriend brings you a mug of tea. Stretches it out in offering. See, he says, nodding toward the mountains. It's not so bad.

And you know, in time, it will be better.

2

Birds of Passage

LYNNE BOWEN

Witnesses made it sound as if it were the beginning of a folk tale: work-weary miners at the end of their shift, wearing mismatched pants and jackets, their faces smudged with coal dust, sing in harmony as they trudge between the rows of shacks in a New World mining town. But the people in the houses they pass do not wave or call out to them as they walk by. The onlookers only listen and watch. The singers are Italian—and they are pariahs.

It is late in the 1880s on Vancouver Island, and the town is called Union Camp. Fifty houses newly built from split logs line either side of the road. In contrast to the surrounding dark forest, whitewash brightens their exterior walls. When the skies clear in the summer of 1889 and the long days are dry and warm, one unidentified Italian is reminded of Italy, where he has left his family to get by until he can send them money.

ABOVE The company-built "camp houses" of Union, the early settlement named after Union Collieries, c. 1889. The Italians who lived at the far end of Union Camp would sing on their way home after their shifts in the Cumberland coal mines. CUMBERLAND MUSEUM & ARCHIVES COLLECTION, C290-001

The houses are newly built because the owner of the company has only recently decided to mine the coal that lies below the ground. Robert Dunsmuir has been acquiring coal leases from prospectors who could not afford to transport the coal to market. Only Mr. Dunsmuir has the capital to do that. Over the previous twenty years the former indentured miner has turned his discovery of the Wellington coal seam near Nanaimo into an empire of mines and railways. And now he is building himself a castle in Victoria.

It is the age of the robber baron, and some would say that Dunsmuir fits the definition: an industrialist who uses ruthless methods to amass wealth. He is a Scot who was raised to value independence, and he will have nothing to do with workers who want a union. His views are well known and have been quoted in newspapers as recently as January of this same year, when a delegation representing striking Wellington miners met with him in Victoria. In the account of the meeting in the January 10 and 11, 1889, issues of the *Daily Colonist*, he is quoted as saying "[T]ell those men that I am a stubborn Scotchman, and that a multitude cannot coerce me or drive me."

ABOVE Company housing lines the railway through the area now known as Camp Road, 1889. The Cumberland townsite was built just to the east in the 1890s, with Dunsmuir Avenue eventually replacing the rail line as the first street in the village.
COURTESY OF THE ROYAL BC MUSEUM, A-04531

Within three months of that meeting Dunsmuir was dead, but before his unexpected demise he had decreed that when he began to develop Comox Valley coal, he would hire only trustworthy miners, men who would cause him as little trouble as possible. By this he meant the hundreds of Chinese workers who were indentured to him because he had paid their head tax, a punitive levy inflicted by Ottawa to discourage Chinese immigration. Under pressure at a protest meeting of Nanaimo and Wellington miners, who unjustly blamed Chinese miners for two horrendous explosions that took the lives of over two hundred men, Dunsmuir and the manager of the Nanaimo mines had agreed to ban the Chinese miners from their underground workings. Dunsmuir moved his Chinese employees to the Comox Valley to build the railway that would transport the coal to a deepwater shipping point at Union Bay.

Dunsmuir also valued Italians, but for a different reason: Italians were known continent-wide as strikebreakers. Ever since Italy had transformed itself from a collection of disparate regions into a unified country in 1870, its government had been unable to deal effectively with a raft of problems, many of which affected the peasantry: inheritance laws that compelled a man to divide his property between all his heirs, rather than leaving all the land to one heir; land that had been degraded by natural disasters and poor farming methods; unemployment and high taxes that made it impossible for a man to support his family—unless he found work elsewhere in the world, some place where men with strong backs but little education could earn enough to allow them to send money home.

A growing number of Italian immigrants, many hired as strikebreakers, had appeared on Vancouver Island starting in the 1870s. Like the Chinese, the Italians were sojourners or, as the poets would say, birds of passage: men who had left their families in their home country and intended to return as soon as they had saved enough money to buy land. Without their families present, these Italians had little stake in the New World communities in which they found work.

Dunsmuir liked to hire Chinese men because they worked for half the wages of other men. He liked to hire Italians because they would dig coal even when other miners refused to work, and he had been hiring them for years. When the Wellington miners went on strike in 1877 to protest Dunsmuir's decision to pay them twenty cents less per ton, he ordered in strikebreakers from San Francisco. His son, James, when testifying later at magistrate's court about their arrival, referred to the newly hired men as "Italians," even though there were also English, French, and Irish strikebreakers among the newcomers who disembarked at Departure Bay.

Not three years later, the manager of the rival coal-mining company in Nanaimo wrote the following to his superiors in London, England, when the company's mines were threatened with a strike: "There is I believe a good many Italians in San Francisco, and many of them are good miners, and if we find it necessary to get fresh hands, I think we should try them, as they are a class that would not be easily advised or intimidated."

The manager's name was John Bryden. Shortly after writing this letter, he resigned his post in Nanaimo and began to work in

Wellington for Dunsmuir, who also happened to be his father-in-law. They were both Ayrshiremen, Scots with a similar attitude toward unions, and it seems they were of like mind when it came to Italians.

Three years into the operation of the mines in the Comox Valley, there were many men in Union Camp who would work for the Dunsmuirs. According to the Dominion census, 231 of the 576 residents were Chinese, and at least 41 were Italian. Both groups lived separately: the Chinese in a sprawling settlement below Union Camp and the Italians at the far end of the camp.

The census information is not precise. What was a Dominion census-taker to make of the person whose name sounded Italian but who said he was born in Austria? All the Italian immigrants at that time were from Piedmont and Lombardy, regions in the northwest corner of Italy that shared a border with the vast Austro-Hungarian Empire. As late as the end of the Second World War, the border between Austria and Italy was frequently disputed and almost as frequently altered by treaty. So, a true-blue Italian could easily have been born in Austrian territory. And just to complicate the census, there were women in Union Camp in 1891 who had Italian names but had been born in Scotland and were Italian only because they had married a man from Italy.

But there was no doubt about the nationality of Pietro Bono. He was born and raised with sixteen siblings in Castellamonte, a farming community near Turin, the capital of Piedmont. Like most Italian emigrants, Pietro was not a miner before he left home, but when he followed his married sister to Union Camp in 1891, the only way for him to earn a living was to dig coal.

Once he had established an income, the next step for a dutiful Italian Catholic bachelor was to marry. There were few Italian women in this New World town when he arrived, but that was about to change, as a worldwide economic depression was causing more women to leave Italy and join their husbands in the New World. Men with families present have a stake in their community and are no longer immune to the ostracism that comes with being a strikebreaker. The typical Italian peasant abroad was evolving from sojourner to permanent immigrant and from strikebreaker to union man.

As was the case with many Italian immigrant men, it is likely that Pietro left it up to his mother to find him a bride in Castellamonte. Giovanna Cerutti was twenty-two when she left the village to marry Pietro, who was ten years her senior. She probably embarked from Genoa and sailed across the Atlantic Ocean to the harbour at New York, where she registered at the Ellis Island immigration processing station in October 1897. Within a month she had travelled across the continent to Vancouver Island to marry Pietro; within a year they were the parents of the first of their nine children.

It cannot have been easy for a newly arrived immigrant woman who did not speak English to adapt to marriage and her new surroundings. Many Italian women in those early days never learned to speak English. But soon there were enough women living in the Italian enclave for them to find companionship and receive help when they gave birth to their children or prepared their dead for burial. Giovanna not only learned to speak English but also became a midwife. All the babies were delivered by midwives in Union Camp, but according to Giovanna's daughter Marie, "If anything went wrong they would always come to my mother."

Giovanna would have need of all her practical knowledge. She gave birth to nine children in eighteen years and then lost Pietro to a mysterious poisoning. Although she fought to have the company admit responsibility for her husband's death, she was never given any monetary help to raise her large family. Instead, she leaned on her own resourcefulness, selling milk from the family cows and sewing for other families. Each of her children went to work at age twelve and, in time-honoured fashion in coal-mining towns the continent over, she allowed her young sons to work in the mines.

The community at the far end of Union Camp was a comforting place for Italians to live and a magnet for certain members of the non-Italian community who liked to play *tressette* in the hall the Italians had built with volunteer labour. They had built a bocce green too, and the shouts of players could be heard throughout the camp when a green ball hit a red ball close to the *pallino*. There were Sunday dances in the hall and impromptu band concerts on the green, as the members of the first of several Italian bands came together to make music.

A combination of separation and cooperation existed between the Italians and the rest of the community. Dorothy Maxwell Graham was a friend of Marie Bono's in later years, but she described the relationship between the two groups in this way: "We didn't go into their houses . . . but my goodness we all went to school together . . . attended the same things and everything like that."

The Ministry of Mines tally of Union Colliery employees for 1891 shows 270 men from various European countries, two hundred men from China, one hundred men from Japan, and a small number of African Americans. All the Europeans except the Italians lived at the near end of Union Camp; the Chinese, Japanese, and African Americans each lived in separate communities.

By this time, after three years of operation, mining activity had reached industrial levels of production. Before the end of the century, surveyors were marking out streets and avenues beyond the camp and civic-minded people were agitating for a new name for the settlement and for municipal incorporation. In 1898, the post office adopted the name Cumberland in recognition of the county in England that matched the town in the Comox Valley in terms of its abundance of coal and beautiful scenery.

It did not take long for Cumberland to become a proper town, with hotels (also known as boarding houses), churches, a graded school, and a newspaper. And even though the newspaper seemed to be going through an identity crisis as it changed its name from *The Weekly News* to *The News* to *The Cumberland News*, it reflected the changing attitude toward Italians under whichever name it was using. The failure of the March 18, 1899,

ABOVE Italian men take a break beside the bocce court at the far end of Union Camp, c. 1904. CUMBERLAND MUSEUM & ARCHIVES COLLECTION, C260-013

edition to identify injured Japanese and Italian miners by name, for example, must have prompted complaints, because the November 25, 1899, issue contained an apology for neglecting to name the Italian man whose ankle had been crushed while he was working in a mine. No such apology was made for not naming the Japanese man whose back had been broken.

The 1901 census shows there were 1,881 people living in Cumberland, at least 111 of whom were Italian. The body count after an explosion in Number Six Mine in February of that year revealed a macabre cross-section of the ethnic origins of the workers: thirty-five Chinese and nine Japanese miners died along with twenty white men, one-quarter of whom were Italian.

Nine years before, twenty-two-year-old Giovanni Marocchi had been left with a permanent limp when a fall of rock broke his leg in Number One Slope. The injury prompted him and his twenty-six-year-old brother, Luis, to leave coal mining and go into business—a transition that would become common for Italian immigrants in the years to come. Marocchi family lore says Giovanni and Luis, both of whom were born in Austria, came to Cumberland in 1886, but their names do not appear in the 1891 census in either Wellington or Union Camp. The indisputable fact is that the Marocchi brothers, using the English versions of their names, John and Louis, became well known as the founders in 1892 of the Marocchi Bakery. The two brothers went back to Italy to fetch Louis's wife, Rosa, to help in the bakery; within two years of their return, Rosa and Louis were the parents of a son they named John Lewis.

The acquisition of a wholesale liquor licence enhanced their profits, enabling them to buy barrels of rum and rye for bottling and to become agents for a beer and porter supplier. That Union Camp had been founded as a temperance community was soon forgotten. The sale of alcohol gave birth to all manner of folk tales, as the Marocchis made it possible for secret drinkers to disguise their liquor purchases and for government agents to be bamboozled during the brief period when Canada experimented with prohibition.

But success in business could not shield them from tragedy. One day, not long after the brothers acquired their liquor licence, they were driving a wagon loaded with hay to feed their delivery horse. The wagon tipped over, spilling the load and throwing Louis to the ground. He died as a result of his injuries, leaving Rosa a widow and six-year-old John Lewis an orphan. Rosa stayed in Cumberland to work in the bakery and later married her brother-in-law, John, making him John Lewis's stepfather.

The first Italian-owned business in Cumberland was eventually able to bake two thousand loaves of bread a day and supply the entire valley, even beyond Union Bay. The aroma of the baking bread filled the air every morning for blocks around, including in Chinatown. And the bread gave John Lewis a story to tell when riots that started in Cumberland spread to all the coal-mining communities of Vancouver Island in 1913.

It happened in midsummer, halfway through what came to be known as the Big Strike of 1912–1914. The long-time battle for union recognition on the Island had a new leader in the United

Mine Workers of America (UMWA). Knowing that there were enough Italians working in Island mines to threaten the success of such a battle, the union had made plans to deal with the problem of Italian strikebreakers. The likelihood that the presence of Italian strikebreakers might mean that the union would lose the battle was more than a faint possibility. A few years later, in the book *The Italian Emigration of Our Times*, Robert Foerster described how Italian strikebreakers helped defeat the Pennsylvania coal strike in 1887 and how even in 1919, when his book was published, only a fraction of Italian coal miners were union members: "In many quarters their early strike-breaking history still condemns them and their competition is feared even when it is not detected." In 1913, the man in charge of assessing the Italian threat on the Island for the UMWA was Joe Angelo. He could be seen in the various Island towns assessing the situation just before tempers erupted in the August heat.

The riots began in Cumberland and spread down Island to all the other communities where miners lived and worked. To restore order, the provincial government called in one thousand militia men. John Lewis Marocchi was seventeen that summer, and he liked to tell the story about delivering bread to the soldiers who were camped on the Cumberland football grounds. Marocchi did not know what to expect as he approached the sentry, who stopped him and demanded, "Advance and be identified." Mustering his courage, John Lewis answered, "The man with the bread." Soon he would be the man in uniform when he joined the Canadian armed forces to serve during the First World War.

The two-year-long strike sputtered to a close when the UMWA withdrew strike pay from the Vancouver Island strikers, and then the war pulled the soldiers away to the battlefields of Europe. The union failed to gain recognition that year, but the failure had nothing to do with the Italians.

During the war, a union man named Albert "Ginger" Goodwin became well known. He had belonged to the union during the strike, and he became notorious when he went to Trail, BC, as a union organizer, having been deemed unfit for military service because of his bad lungs and rotten teeth. But when he became troublesome in Trail, the authorities declared him to be fit for military service. He fled Trail and took refuge in the mountains behind Comox Lake near Cumberland, where sympathetic local people supplied him with the necessities of life.

Ginger became a legend when he was shot in the back and killed by a Dominion Police constable, and at that point his story merges with the Italian story. Workers from all over the province held a one-day general strike to mark his funeral, and the procession of mourners that stretched behind the white coffin from one end of Dunsmuir Avenue to the other was led by the West Cumberland Band, better known as the Italian Band.

The Italian Band in all its versions had been an important part of the Cumberland scene since it was founded in 1891. Incomplete records show that when Paolo Monte founded the Italian Band "just for fun," it was before 1906, and though the members are said to have been dispersed just before the Big Strike, the Italian Band certainly existed in 1918 when it led Ginger's funeral procession.

The ebullient Paolo, known for his showmanship, stayed in Cumberland for only a few years, but his brass band had become an essential part of Cumberland's social life, as the musicians accompanied Sunday dances at the Italian Hall, serenaded picnickers on their way to Millard Beach, and provided the marching beat for parades down Dunsmuir Avenue.

On August 2, 1918, the Italian Band led hundreds of mourners to the cemetery to witness the burial of Ginger Goodwin. The grave remained unmarked by a headstone until the 1930s, when Vincent Picketti, an Italian trained in the old-world art of stonemasonry, sliced off a section of a large boulder and inscribed it with Ginger's name and the motto A Worker's Friend.

The Cumberland burial ground is divided by a highway now: Chinese and Japanese graves are on one side, Europeans on the other. On the European side, as in many North American cemeteries, believers are buried in separate Protestant and Catholic sections. In the oldest rows of the Catholic section, many of the headstones bear Italian names: families from the earliest days of mining and the victims of the 1901 explosion in Number Six Mine. These were the workers who, along with the Chinese, were preferred by Robert Dunsmuir in 1888.

The difference between the fates of Italian and Chinese birds of passage came down to family. Until 1947, when the *Chinese Immigration Act* of 1923 was repealed, very few Chinese women were allowed to come to Canada. They saw their husbands only when the men returned to China for a visit. There was no law to deter Italian family reunification, however, and as early as the 1890s, Italian women began to join their husbands in the Comox Valley. With the women came the desire to become members of the new community. Italians' love of *la familia* was mainly responsible for ending the Italian connection to strikebreaking.

SOURCES

ANNUAL REPORTS OF THE MINISTRY OF MINES. Victoria, BC: Royal British Columbia Archives, 1888–1901.

BOWEN, LYNNE. *Robert Dunsmuir, Laird of the Mines*. Montreal, Quebec: XYZ Publishing, 1999.

BOWEN, LYNNE. *Three Dollar Dreams*. Lantzville, BC: Oolichan Books, 1987.

BOWEN, LYNNE. *Those Island People*. Nanaimo, BC: Rocky Point Books, 2013.

BOWEN, LYNNE. *Whoever Gives Us Bread: The Story of Italians in British Columbia*. Vancouver, BC: Douglas & McIntyre, 2011.

BRITISH COLUMBIA. Division of Vital Statistics. Registration of Births, Deaths, and Marriages Act, 1889–1911. Microfilm, Royal British Columbia Archives.

CONTI, MARIE, DOROTHY GRAHAM, AND JOHN MAROCCHI. Interviewed on February 2, 1984, by Lynne Bowen in Cumberland, BC. VIURRSpace. http://hdl.handle.net/10613/129

CUMBERLAND WEEKLY NEWS (also known as *The Weekly News* and *The News*) 1897–1901. https://open.library.ubc.ca/collections/bcnewspapers/xcumberland

DAILY COLONIST. January 10 and 11, 1889. https://newspaperarchive.com/search/location/ca/bc/victoria/victoria-daily-colonist/1889/

DUNCAN, ERIC. *Fifty-Seven Years in the Comox Valley*. Comox: J. Barrett Gilmour, 1967.

FOERSTER, ROBERT F. *The Italian Emigration of Our Times*. London: Oxford University Press, 1919.

MAROCCHI, RAY. Telephone interview in March 2004 with Lynne Bowen.

MAYSE, SUSAN. *Ginger: The Life and Death of Albert Goodwin*. Madeira Park: Harbour Publishing, 1990.

NANAIMO DAILY FREE PRESS, February 26, 1877. Koerner Library, University of British Columbia, AW1 .R-13, Microfilm. https://webcat.library.ubc.ca/vwebv/holdingsInfo?bibId=1223479

"PASSENGER SEARCH," The Statue of Liberty—Ellis Island Foundation, https://heritage.statueofliberty.org/passenger.

PLOT PLAN OF CEMETERY. Cumberland Museum and Archives.

PORTER, BRIAN J. "British Columbia's Mining Casualties," *British Columbia Genealogist*, Part One, 9, no. 1 (Spring 1980); Part Two, 9, no. 2 (Summer 1980); Part Three (with Alice Marwood), 9, no. 3 (Fall 1980); Parts Four and Five, 9, no. 4 (Winter 1980).

"UNION CITY AND COLLIERY, Vancouver Island, 1889." *British Columbia Genealogist* 7, no. 3–4 (extracted from the *Nanaimo Free Press*, August 10, 1889, edition). Vancouver Public Library. https://webcat.library.ubc.ca/vwebv/holdingsInfo?bibId=1223479

VANCOUVER COAL MINING AND LAND COMPANY. "Diary and Letterbook," 1878-1880. Royal British Columbia Archives.

VANCOUVER ISLAND HISTORICAL CENSUS DATA. See hcmc.uvic.ca/project/vicensus/index.html

"For several, horror-filled seconds, the appalled fireman stared into the chasm below, smoke and dust billowing upward and about him. Peering into the gloom, Piercy called again and again for his comrades. But there was no answer beyond the death groans of the train." *DAILY COLONIST*, AUGUST 18, 1974

3

Tides of Time

KIM BANNERMAN

I'm not where I thought I'd be.

Growing up near the river and naturally drawn to thrilling disaster stories, I've always been fascinated by the Trent River Train Disaster. On the morning of August 17, 1898, a train pulling twenty cars and carrying nine passengers plunged off a collapsing 100-foot span of the Trent River trestle, located between Cumberland and Union Bay.

What a wonderful opportunity this book presents to write about this particular tragedy! As part of my research, I initially planned to hike along the Trent River and look for any remaining evidence of the event, but to be honest, I didn't expect there would be much left to see. It's been over a century since the bridge fractured and fell, and the tides of time are adept at washing away evidence. Still, this project provides an excellent motivation to get off the couch, and I was certain it would make a fun hike. At the very least, it would provide exercise and fresh air, a welcome change after weeks of digging through musty old newspaper articles. If I was lucky, perhaps I'd spot the last crumbled bit of footings where the old trestle once stood.

Two workmen were examining those very footings on that fateful August morning when they heard a crack, like the blast of a rifle, from above their heads. They looked up just in time to see the bridge collapsing directly over them. Both men sprang out of the way as the train engine, wooden beams, coal cars, and crew tumbled out of the sky, crashing into the middle of the dry ravine and transforming into a heap of twisted debris, burning coal, and broken bodies. Only one man from the train was unscathed. Matt Piercy, the second brakeman, had been riding on the rear car when he heard the crack, and when he looked up, he saw the line of cars before him disappearing, one after the other, over the side. He was the only man able to leap to safety.

In 1898, newspapers were the vehicle for most information up and down the coast, and both the Cumberland *News* and Victoria *Daily Colonist* ran extensive columns about the event. Testimony from the three witnesses framed the story and provided gruesome details for inquisitive readers. The *Daily Colonist* reported "a grinding and splintering of timbers, a crash, a plunge of heavy bodies, a sound of rushing steam, and a chorus of shrieks as men were hurried into eternity." Sensationalism in the media is not a new phenomenon.

The dramatic tableau of shattered wreckage and broken beams scattered across the bottom of a dusty riverbed piqued my interest, so I searched through the old articles, plotted my ideas, and decided to visit the ravine. I hoped to capture a glimpse of that sweltering, sticky, and smoke-filled canyon on that distant summer morning and get a sense of how difficult it must have been for people to relay messages, get help, administer first aid to the wounded, and collect the dead.

But—as I said—that's not where I find myself. I'm not standing at the bridge footings, nor anywhere near the ravine. The story has taken a surprising turn, and I'm not where I thought I'd be.

ABOVE Rescue crews pose on the engine wreckage at the site of the Trent River Train Disaster. CUMBERLAND MUSEUM & ARCHIVES COLLECTION, C285-003

THE ARTICLES PROVED to be invaluable in helping me piece together the lurid details of the incident: the boom of the timbers breaking, the hiss of the steam-wreathed engine plunging through the air, the horror felt by the workmen who impotently watched the horror unfold. In both the *News* and the *Daily Colonist*, most of the crew and passengers are named, along with their family relations, past employment, or reason for travel. For example, Alexander Mellado left a widow and infant; William Work was the son of James Work, another local contractor; and Miss Frances Horne was the daughter of William Horne, a blacksmith who worked at Union Bay. The *News* also included gory descriptions of the grotesque injuries sustained by the victims, which must have been agonizing for family and friends to read. The articles aren't short on details.

Except when it comes to two individuals.

At the close of this lurid list is a tiny sentence informing the public that an additional pair of bodies was pulled from the wreckage. These men were of Japanese ancestry—and they are not named. They are simply lumped together in a category based on race, and no other details are offered.

It was standard practice at the time for newspapers to name only victims who were of European descent. Mining towns in the late 1800s were familiar with disaster, for the jobs were brutal, dangerous, and difficult, and safety measures were often lacking. From explosions to shaft collapses, flooding, or suffocation by gas, newspapers carried multiple reports of death and tragedy, but time and again, articles list endless details about white victims yet read like census tallies for everyone else. Personal information is scant. The *News* offers a minor exception by informing readers that "the two Japanese killed at the bridge accident were buried at the Japanese cemetery. They were followed to their graves by many of their countrymen."

Again, though, no names are shared.

This glaring omission speaks to how immigrant workers were treated, how people of Asian descent were considered by those of European descent, and how the company viewed their employees. Trawling through the newspapers, a quick sweep of the columns reveals ugly, racist attitudes. Articles and advertisements are filled with comments and stereotypes that make the blood boil and teeth clench—and that regrettably aren't so different from the hate-fuelled vitriol that still appears today online, pitting one group against another. The removal of an individual's identity has long been used as a weapon to dehumanize and demean, to strip away dignity. It encourages readers to nurture an "us vs. them" philosophy and destroys the ability to make meaningful connections with people, both in contemporary accounts and in the annals of history. Our name is a reflection of our humanity.

But if the newspapers did not, would not, identify these two individuals, perhaps other sources did.

A local history blog compiled by Robin Shaw suggests that the names were recorded elsewhere, perhaps in legal documents. I began to search through an online legal database that lists Supreme Court of Canada cases reaching back to 1877. Tucked away in this list of judgements is the case of *Union Colliery Co. v. The Queen*, dated December 7, 1900. The company had been indicted for unlawfully causing death by neglecting to maintain the bridge; at the trial, a guilty verdict had been entered, and the defendants were convicted and ordered to pay a fine of five thousand dollars. However, the defendants appealed on the question reserved for the opinion of the court: "Will the indictment lie against a corporation?" and followed with the statement, "If this question be answered in the negative, the conviction is to be quashed; otherwise, the conviction is to stand."

As Judge J. Sedgewick stated during the appeal, "'Everyone' is an expression of the same kind as 'person,' and therefore includes bodies corporate unless the context requires otherwise. There is no doubt that the expression 'every one' [*sic*] is, whether in a legal or popular sense, a wider term than the word 'person,' . . . There can be no question that the word 'person' may, and I should be disposed myself to say *primâ facie* does, in a public statute, include a person in law; that is, a corporation, as well as a natural person."

The jury at the appeal came to the conclusion that a corporation should be considered an entity bound by law in the same way that a "natural person" is bound, and the appeal was dismissed.

In the middle of this document, the employees who lost their lives are listed: "Alfred Walker, Richard Nightingale, Walter Work, Alexander Mellodo [*sic*], K. Nanko (Japanese), and Osana (Japanese)."

SO, WHILE I ORIGINALLY planned to visit the site of the train disaster, I instead find myself at Nikkei No Haka, which roughly translates as "Grave of the Immigrants" and is also known as Cumberland Japanese cemetery. It's located on a knoll above a stretch of wetlands east of town, near enough to the main highway that the hum of traffic remains constant behind the sounds of birdsong and creaking branches. Despite the parade of eighteen-wheelers roaring nearby, it is a serene and tranquil place. The spring afternoon is pleasant and warm. The first trilliums of the season are visible in the marshy ground, and the tips of the conifers are bright lime-green with new growth. High above me, hidden

ABOVE Cumberland's Japanese graveyard in 1901. CUMBERLAND MUSEUM & ARCHIVES COLLECTION, C140-370

in the branches, a raven croaks and laughs, then swoops away with the whisper of mighty wings. Shafts of sunlight slant down through the majestic hemlocks. The ground is illuminated by soft stripes of green and gold.

Approximately two hundred people are buried on this sacred slope of land established as a cemetery in 1895. Between the trees, the square outlines of graves appear muted with plush carpets of moss, half-hidden under vibrant banks of waxy salal leaves. The cemetery was dedicated as a heritage landmark in 2008, and every August, a Buddhist minister from Steveston performs a special ceremony called Obon, which acknowledges and honours the people buried here.

Unlike other graveyards, where headstones are spaced in long straight rows, the headstones in Nikkei No Haka are clustered together at the top of the hill, carefully set in a circle under the sheltering boughs. The stones seem to gather in the round, seeking comfort in each other's company.

The Cumberland *News* states that the men were buried here on August 18, the Thursday following the train accident, and I hope to find some hint of their names on the stones—and perhaps discover the full first name of "K." Nanko.

However, I'm severely hampered by three undeniable facts:

1. I can't read Japanese. I have scrawled the characters for each name on a piece of paper, and I am slowly tracing my way through each stone, but there is no guarantee that I, in my ignorance, won't scan over and miss what I'm looking for. I am an illiterate idiot fumbling from sigil to sigil, and I curse myself for not taking Japanese lessons in high school.
2. Time has not been kind to these headstones. Many of the oldest stones are carved from sandstone and slate, which are both readily available in this mountainous landscape but hardly durable. Like boulders at the shore of the ocean, they're weather-worn and soft-edged, eroded by the constant tides of time. If the names were ever here, 120 years may have erased them.
3. Most importantly, this shrine of clustered headstones does not reflect their original placement, and not all headstones that once stood in this cemetery have survived.

Here, the events of the twentieth century intrude upon those of the nineteenth century, tripping up the efforts of a modern researcher firmly planted in the twenty-first.

Hatred for the enemy during the Second World War ignited bitter acts of racism along the West Coast, and the Japanese internment experience continues to be a painful scar on living memory. In addition to the large communities of Japanese Canadians at both No. 5 Townsite and No. 1 Townsite, the Royston Lumber mill employed more than one hundred Japanese mill workers. After the Canadian government forcibly relocated these families to internment camps in British Columbia's Interior, this graveyard became a focal point for violence and resentment. In the years following internment, the headstones were toppled and smashed, left to be forgotten among the moss and ferns. Once again, we find the living attempting to erase the names of the dead. A corporation may have been seen as a "natural person," but that same courtesy was not extended to those who were born, lived, and died on this soil, and who contributed to the growth and development of the city of Cumberland.

For more than twenty years, the stones lay silent among the grass and ferns. Then, in 1967, volunteers resurrected those markers that remained intact. With no way of knowing which stones matched which grave, they gathered them together to create a poignant memorial and let the land over the graves grow natural and wild.

As the afternoon sun traces its journey through the sky, my futile search for the names on the stones becomes an act of reflection. My mind wanders. Perhaps K. Nanko and Osana came here as *dekasegi rodo*, single men from Japan who worked in foreign countries, earning money to save for their future and always keeping in their heart the intention to return home. Or perhaps they had hoped to stay here and make Cumberland their home, to find a place where they could raise families, helping to establish neighbourhoods in No. 5 Townsite, in No. 1 Townsite, and around the Royston Lumber Mill. I want to know more about them. I want to learn about their dreams and their hopes, the people they loved and who loved them in return.

"All the district is naturally thrown into the deepest sorrow, and the families of the victims of the tragedy have the sincerest sympathy of the entire community," stated the *Daily Colonist* on August 18, 1898. In the Cumberland *News*, only two days later, one reads, "Heaped high above [the coffin] were gifts of flowers, the best that friendship could offer. People came—more than the little cottage could hold—came, and went to make room for others." But the newspapers describe only the funerals of white male victims. I want to know how K. Nanko and Osana were celebrated at the end of their lives, and who remembered them with fondness and devotion.

However, I have not been able to find out more about these two men. I don't know if any other records of their existence remain, and those who have chronicled the twentieth century have been nasty to the subjects they considered unworthy of remembrance.

Like the footings of the bridge—which crumbled under their burden yet remain visible to those who know the river's history—one has only to look around this beautiful place to recognize the lasting impact of racism here and how it shaped the formation of this graveyard, this town, this community, this country.

Perhaps, by discussing the darkest acts of Cumberland's diverse history, we can learn how to create a more welcoming and resilient future, where the contributions of each individual are equally celebrated and remembered, regardless of class, status, gender, or race. In writing this piece, I'm not where I thought I'd be, but that's okay: this essay took me to a place where I need to be. In some small way, remembering K. Nanko and Osana alongside the other victims of the Trent River Train Disaster provides a hint of all that we've collectively lost due to unkindness, cruelty, or misrepresentation. And perhaps, despite the newspapers' attempts to reduce them to a single forgettable line, we can snatch their names back from the tides of time, drag them back onto the sunlit shore, and honour their place in the foundations of Cumberland's history.

SOURCES

COPEMAN, D. "Hidden Treasures." *CV Collective Magazine* (Fall 2016). https://thecollectivemags.ca/hidden-treasures/

SHAW, ROBIN L. A. "Trent River Train Disaster." *Comox Valley, Vancouver Island, and More* (blog). http://beautifulcomoxvalley.blogspot.com/p/the-trent-river-train-disaster-is-one.html

THE NEWS. "Bridge Disaster." August 20, 1898, p. 1. https://open.library.ubc.ca/viewer/xcumberland/1.0176408#p0z-3r0f

UNION COLLIERY CO. V. THE QUEEN, [1900] 31 SCR 81. https://scc-csc.lexum.com/scc-csc/scc-csc/en/item/7666/index.do?q=Personne+b

VANCOUVER ISLAND 1891 CENSUS. *viHistory*. https://hcmc.uvic.ca/~taprhist/content/census/1891/census1891.php?page=subdistricts#:~:text=In%20the%201891%20census%2C%20the%20population%20of%20the%20district%20was%2017%2C998

VICTORIA DAILY COLONIST. "The Bridge Gave Way." August 18, 1898, p. 2. https://archive.org/details/dailycolonist18980818uvic/page/n1/mode/2up?view=theater

4

Joe Naylor

Workers' Rights and a Better World

ROD MICKLEBURGH

The story is told of a group of young English lads wandering the countryside long ago, cold and hungry, looking for work, when an ornate coach stopped alongside them. A well-dressed gentleman leaned out the door to wish them a good day. Several doffed their hats and bowed. Joe Naylor did not. "You're fools," he told his mates. "Why should starving men bow and scrape to this popinjay? If he truly meant well, he would work to help right the country's wrongs." The door slammed shut and the carriage quickly moved on, leaving the boys a little colder and a little hungrier.

The tale may well be apocryphal, but it was told years later by none other than Joe Naylor himself. True or not, it showcased the class consciousness and the drive to fight for workers' rights and a better world that characterized Naylor's life from a young age to his death in 1946 at age seventy-four. For the last half of his radical life, he lived in Cumberland.

ABOVE This portrait of labour activist Joe Naylor, a glass-plate negative taken at the Hayashi Studio in Cumberland c. 1929, is one of the only known photos of him. CUMBERLAND MUSEUM & ARCHIVES COLLECTION, 987.019.182

The tough, gritty aspects of the town so familiar to early residents like Naylor are mostly gone from Cumberland today. The storied old village has been quietly redefining itself as a laid-back, hipsters' haven and a neighbourly place to raise a family. One has to look hard to find traces of its long history, dominated by coal mining, a harsh, exploitative industry that sparked fierce resistance by local miners against the unscrupulous pit owners, whose fortunes were made by the miners' sweat and toil.

The height of this resistance coincided with Naylor's first years in Cumberland, during the second decade of the twentieth century. This was the time of the Great Vancouver Island Coal Strike (1912–1914), the most protracted, violent strike in BC history, the shooting of labour leader Ginger Goodwin in rugged terrain outside Cumberland (1918), and the Winnipeg General Strike (1919). Socialists were regularly elected to the BC legislature, and industrial workers across the West, including in Cumberland, rushed to join the One Big Union (OBU), as radical a union movement as Canada has ever seen, formed just after the Winnipeg General Strike.

Joe Naylor was at the forefront of much of this activity, to such an extent that the North-West Mounted Police (NWMP) dispatched a permanent, undercover operative to Cumberland to keep an eye on him. In a "secret and confidential report," BC's E Division told the commissioner of the NWMP that "Joseph Naylor is well known in these parts, and I am of the opinion that his removal at some time would have a most beneficial effect."

A century later, however, the story of this remarkable man has mostly been forgotten, even in his home community. For years, his final resting spot in the Cumberland cemetery was marked only by a small metal plaque, a humble contrast to the imposing nearby gravestone of his former comrade-in-arms, Ginger Goodwin.

His gravesite was upgraded in 1997 to a standing rock with a brass plaque and poem. But while there is an annual pilgrimage to Goodwin's grave on Cumberland's Miners Memorial Weekend,

Naylor's grave attracts relatively little notice, beyond brief mentions and the laying of individual flowers. Given the nature of Goodwin's death at the age of just thirty-one, this is understandable. Martyrs live on, ever young. Goodwin gave his life for justice and workers' rights. A mountain and a section of highway have been named after him, and he is rightfully celebrated in song, books, and a play. But would Ginger Goodwin have become as famous without the mentorship of Joe Naylor?

When Goodwin showed up in Cumberland to work the mines, just before the strike began in 1912, Naylor headed both the local branch of the Socialist Party of Canada and Local 2299 of the United Mine Workers of America (UMWA). Despite their fifteen-year age gap, Naylor took the younger Goodwin under his wing, and they became fast friends. They fished for trout, attended local dances, and shared a love of soccer. It doesn't seem a stretch to suggest that Goodwin's subsequent championing of Socialism and trade unionism was fired by his older, more experienced friend.

SOCIALIST, PACIFIST, ORGANIZER, beacon of racial tolerance, comrade, leader, and teacher, Joe Naylor was a modest, principled, and unrelenting advocate for the working class and an end to "this damnable system." He left an indelible mark on BC labour history. Naylor was, says the historian Roger Stonebanks, the most radical union leader on Vancouver Island and one of the province's most prominent militants.

His best-known photo, taken by the resident photographer Senjiro Hayashi, shows a thickset, serious-looking individual with thinning hair and a finely trimmed moustache.

Born in 1872, Naylor grew up in Wigan, a bleak industrial town in Lancashire, in the northwest of England, dominated by cotton mills and coal mines where child labour and appalling working conditions were rife. The town later became well known for the wrong reasons in the 1930s, when author George Orwell highlighted the area in *The Road to Wigan Pier*, his book about Britain's grinding, working-class poverty.

A working miner almost all his life, Naylor first worked underground as a pit lad. He may have started as young as ten, the minimum age for employment in Victorian Britain. Though many mines were unionized, conditions remained grim. Lancashire miners laboured for some of the lowest pay in the country, their lives constantly at risk from underground hazards. Naylor stuck it out as long as he could, but eventually he joined hundreds of thousands of other British coal miners who abandoned their jobs and set out for what they hoped would be a better life in North America. His first stop was Butte, Montana, in 1908. There, the ore fields were so rich and the jobs so plentiful that many immigrants were told when they arrived on the east coast: "Don't stop in America. Go straight to Butte." It was also a radical union hotbed, where Socialists, Wobblies (members of the Industrial Workers of the World), and the militant Western Federation of Miners held sway, fighting pitched battles against the copper bosses. Despite the political and union fervour, however, Naylor did not stay long. Perhaps he missed living under the Union Jack. The next year he crossed the border and found work in the coal mines of Cumberland.

IT'S DIFFICULT TO IMAGINE how much of the economy of touristy, picturesque Vancouver Island once relied on coal, the dirtiest of all fossil fuels and the most dangerous to mine. For more than fifty years, Ladysmith, Nanaimo, the mostly lost communities of Extension and Wellington, and Cumberland were coal-mining communities, with black dust in the air, small bungalows and bunkhouses for the miners, and regular processions to the cemetery to bury victims of mining disasters.

The loss of life was horrendous. An 1887 explosion in Nanaimo that claimed 150 lives remains Canada's second-deadliest mining disaster. Seven months later, another explosion took seventy-seven lives. On February 15, 1901, a series of blasts ripped through Mine No. 6 in Cumberland, killing sixty-four miners. After yet another disaster, a miner's wife lamented, bitterly,

"You don't forget, when you see thirty graves, all new, dug in a row waiting to be filled with men you've known all your life."

And no matter how often Island miners fought for safer working conditions and better pay, they were unable to crack the steadfast anti-unionism of the mining barons. Strike after strike for union recognition ended in defeat. Strikebreakers, the eviction of strikers from their company homes, and all-out support for the owners from the authorities stacked the deck every time. Those who dared to go on strike were blacklisted from future employment. The miners couldn't win.

That was the situation when Joe Naylor arrived in Cumberland in 1909 at the age of thirty-seven, an unwavering Socialist and dedicated trade unionist. His new home proved fertile ground. The Socialist Party of Canada had a strong following on the Island. The recent provincial election had sent two Socialists to the legislature from Nanaimo. The Socialist candidate in Comox finished second. Naylor was soon recording secretary of the Socialists' Cumberland chapter. Business meetings took place every Sunday morning in the Socialist Hall across from the post office, followed by meatier "propaganda" gatherings in the afternoon devoted to "the principles and programmes of the revolutionary working class." Classes in economics were offered twice a day on Thursdays: at 10:30 a.m. for miners on the afternoon shift and 8:00 p.m. for the morning shift.

It did not take Naylor long to don his trade union hat. In what they saw as one last, no-holds-barred attempt to finally organize the Island's coal mines, the miners had called in the UMWA, a tough, seasoned, well-heeled union, with a long record of taking on ruthless coal companies south of the border. Hundreds began signing up and Naylor was elected president of UMWA Local 2299 in Cumberland.

As the miners prepared for the confrontation they knew was coming, Naylor continued to work shifts in the No. 7 Shaft at nearby Bevan and to pepper the pages of the Socialist paper, the *Western Clarion*, and organized labour's weekly *Federationist* with his forceful opinions. At one point, he denounced the seemingly innocent efforts to form a troop of Boy Scouts. In those days, however, the Scouts included a significant dose of militarism, and members were sometimes schooled in the use of guns and bayonets. Socialists like Naylor were appalled. "Bayonets are made by the working class, nicely polished by the working class, and then patriotically thrust into the working class for the capitalist class," he wrote with a flourish.

THE GREAT COAL STRIKE of 1912–1914 started in Cumberland, when the company fired Oscar Mottishaw, a safety-conscious union miner. Mottishaw had already been let go from the Extension Mine after reporting gas in one of the shafts. Jobless, he managed to find mining work in Cumberland as a mule driver. When the company learned that he was on-site, he was once again sent packing. His dismissal lit the fire for the following two years of bitter confrontation. The next day, September 16, miners in Cumberland and Extension declared a one-day "holiday" and demanded that Mottishaw be re-hired. When they tried to return to work, the owners closed the gates. Sixteen hundred miners were off the job, and the war was on. Naylor later told a royal commission into the causes of the strike that their one-day walkout was only a protest. They had no intention of embarking on anything longer.

But there was no turning back. Striking miners were quickly ousted from their homes. At the same time, the mine owners ensured miners from China and Japan stayed on the job by threatening them with deportation if they, too, walked out. Company police surrounded their living quarters to keep the strikers away. Outside strikebreakers hired by the company to maintain production were also protected. For their part, the miners had the backing of the UMWA, strike pay of four dollars a week, staunch support from their wives, and a rousing solidarity that made life as difficult as possible for the scabs.

Yet eight months into the strike, despite the union's best efforts, the struck mines were nearing normal production. Something had to be done. On May Day 1913, a rip-roaring, jam-packed meeting in Nanaimo unanimously endorsed the union's decision to expand the strike to all three working mines in Nanaimo. The next day, 3,700 miners, from Cumberland to Ladysmith, were out.

Tempers were short. Feelings ran high. But in Cumberland, under Joe Naylor's calming leadership, and in the face of provocation from the scabs and the permanent posting of extra police officers to the community, strikers kept their cool. That changed on July 19, when, according to an account a few weeks later by Bob Walker in the *Western Clarion*, a man identified as Cane led a number of strikebreakers into town to taunt the strikers. When Naylor tried to get him to simmer down, Cane, described by Walker as "a hired thug," challenged him to a fight. A striker rushed forward to belt Cane, and a wild donnybrook ensued. The scabs got the worst of it, and Cane was never seen again, Walker told *Clarion* readers.

Several days after the brawl, in blatant disregard of his peacemaking efforts, Naylor was arrested on a charge of unlawful assembly and thrown in jail. In yet another piece in the *Clarion*, a visitor painted a vivid picture of the accused behind bars: "Joe was pleased to see me. He was cheerful, but a blind man could see that Joe felt like a caged lion. Joe likes to be up and doing. He is one of the most active members of the movement and to be chained up at a time like this is very trying."

He was held without bail for months, which conveniently removed him from his leadership role in the strike at a critical time. When his case came to trial in New Westminster, the charge was thrown out. But the damage had been done.

The mine owners had had their eye on Naylor since the strike began. When the company asked their mine superintendent in Cumberland to name the chief agitators behind the original one-day strike, Naylor headed the list. He was far and away the most popular and influential union leader in Cumberland, respected for his integrity, even by many of the strikebreakers. The *Clarion* didn't mince words about why Naylor was singled out: "Being a class-conscious man, he was naturally a thorn in the side of the capitalists and the obvious prey of the rapacious thugs that are at present infesting the Island."

However, support from trade unionists up and down the Pacific Coast, an inspirational visit from the famous "Miners Angel" Mother Jones, $1.5 million from the UMWA to support the strike, and the immense heart and valour of the miners were simply not enough to overcome the forces arrayed against them. At one point, even the militia was sent in, complete with a Gatling machine gun mounted on the back of a flatbed rail car, to arrest scores of strikers, following a series of embittered attacks against scabs in Ladysmith and Extension.

After two courageous years of struggle, the strike was called off. The union-busting mine owners had won. The mining company's promise not to discriminate against any striker who had worked for them before the walkout began proved as worthless as the paper it wasn't written on. Naylor, Goodwin, and hundreds of other strikers paid a steep price for their resistance.

The mines were closed to Joe Naylor for the next ten years. Unlike Goodwin, who decamped to Trail, Naylor stayed in Cumberland. He survived by living frugally in his small lakeside cabin, fishing, hunting, and working occasionally as an organizer for the UMWA.

Rather than be cowed, Naylor increased his commitment to the cause. In 1917, at the organization's convention in Revelstoke, he was elected president of the BC Federation of Labour as part of a decisive shift to the left. Almost everyone on the new executive was a Socialist, including Naylor and Goodwin, chosen as one of eight vice-presidents. By then the terrible "war to end all wars" was three years old, and few delegates saw it as anything more than pointless carnage, pitting members of the working class against each other for the benefit of profiteers, politicians, and out-of-touch generals. Under Naylor, the Federation took a vigorous stand against military conscription.

The convention also gave Naylor another chance to demonstrate his principled belief that workers from China and Japan should be welcomed, not shunned, by the labour movement. Three years earlier, in 1914, he had stood virtually alone at the Federation's convention to oppose a resolution calling for the exclusion of all Asian workers from BC. Noting that his own local supported it, Naylor nevertheless contended that Cumberland's Chinese and Japanese miners would not have worked during the strike if they had been given a choice. Rejecting an earlier statement that labelled them "the curse of BC," Naylor contended, "It is the white men, especially the men who have come from the same country as myself, that are the real curse in this province. It's not the Asiatics at all!" It cannot be overstated how rare this attitude was in the labour movement of the time.

Now Naylor had his own resolution. He called on the province to impose a minimum wage for all underground miners, regardless of their ethnicity. That, he argued, would end the mine owners' long-standing practice of undercutting wages by paying Asian miners significantly less than white workers. Naylor's views prevailed and the resolution passed.

A YEAR LATER, Goodwin's refusal to be conscripted led to his death. He was shot by a special constable named Dan Campbell close to his Cumberland area hideout. The largest procession in the village's history paraded his white casket through the muddy streets. Joe Naylor was one of three speakers at his funeral. He had already viewed Goodwin's body at the undertakers, taking measurements and making notes about his fatal injury. At a speedily held inquest into Goodwin's death, Naylor, on behalf of the victim's friends and family, asked a series of questions that exposed numerous inconsistencies in testimony by the police and medical investigators. The coroner's jury ignored them, and Campbell subsequently went free.

Goodwin's bid to escape conscription gave authorities one more opportunity to go after Naylor. Two weeks after the inquest, he was arrested again. He was committed for trial in Nanaimo on a charge of aiding draft-evaders by providing them with food and other assistance. It was a serious charge. If convicted, Naylor stood a good chance of being deported, a tactic the federal government was using more and more to rid the country of Socialists and other radicals.

But the attempt to have him jailed and possibly deported went nowhere. Justice Denis Murphy told the Nanaimo jury that the accused was before the court on the "slimmest evidence" he had ever seen put forth for a trial. Jurors agreed it would be a waste of the court's time to proceed, and Naylor was cleared without a formal trial.

As the First World War neared its end in 1918, Naylor decided not to seek re-election as president of the Federation of Labour. Instead, he threw himself into the escalating, quasi-revolutionary battle for worker rights that was sweeping the West.

The movement culminated in the formation of the ultra-militant OBU and the historic Winnipeg General Strike. Naylor's reputation was such that a list compiled by an anti-union Winnipeg newspaper of those believed responsible for agitating local workers to participate in the strike had his name at the top. As absurd as that was, given that he never went near the Manitoba capital, it demonstrated his high profile in the OBU, which the government and Winnipeg business interests blamed for the strike. The OBU called for direct action and general strikes to take on capitalism once and for all. Its mantra was production for use, not for profit.

Unions representing more than forty thousand workers hopped aboard the OBU train. Naylor joined Socialist luminaries William Pritchard and Victor Midgely of Vancouver on the OBU's five-person central committee. He was also secretary of its Vancouver Island branch. "It seems the spirit of unionism is growing on the Island," he wrote in the pages of the *Federationist*. "Dangerous working conditions in the mines could be overturned, if the men, themselves, would only join together in a progressive organization, with the principle imbued within them that 'an injury to one is an injury to all.'"

That sentiment was extended to Chinese and Japanese workers. The OBU echoed Naylor's long-standing support for Asian inclusion, calling on all unions to accept them as members. "It is a class problem, not a race problem that confronts the white worker in BC," proclaimed the OBU.

However, beset by internal squabbling, constant hounding by police, and opposition from mainstream unions, the OBU did not last long. The great wave of radicalism passed, and with it went Naylor's beloved Socialist Party, its platform was eclipsed by a new left-wing party, the Communist Party of Canada. Like many on the left, Naylor was initially drawn to the Russian Revolution and its overthrow of a militarized society that enforced hated conscription. But his interest was short-lived. He remained a Socialist to the end.

The 1920s were tough times for unions. In Cumberland, the mine owners felt secure enough to let Naylor, then in his early fifties, resume his old coal-mining job in 1923. Not until 1937, twenty-three years after the end of the great coal strike, did the UMWA manage to organize Cumberland's mines and sign a contract. At age sixty-five, Naylor had a union job at last.

But the workers of the 1930s were not the combative workers of old, and Naylor did not participate much in the union. When the miners agreed to a wage rollback, however, the old lion roused himself one more time. Recalled his close friend Karl Coe: "He got up on the platform and bawled them out. He says, 'I've never seen such a damned mess in my life. You guys, starving to death, and you give [the mine owners] eight per cent!' Oh, he gave them hell that day."

After a time, Naylor was spared working underground and given an easier job on the coal-picking table. He retired from a lifetime of coal mining in 1943 at the age of seventy-one. In retirement, he continued to live a spartan, bachelor life at his modest cabin on the shores of Comox Lake. There was no shortage of visitors. Bronco Moncrief, who went on to become the mayor of Cumberland for more than thirty years, remembered delivering

ABOVE Joe Naylor died at age seventy-four and was laid to rest beside Albert "Ginger" Goodwin, his protégé. His graveside service was led by Cumberland Local 7293 of the United Mine Workers of America and included a personal tribute by the local president, John Cameron. COURTESY OF ROD MICKLEBURGH, 2015

the *Vancouver Sun* to him in 1942: "He was a big, powerful man and rowed a sixteen-foot boat. My eyes popped out, when he offered me stew and dumplings, warmed up from the day before, for breakfast."

Karl Coe was a frequent visitor. "Many a time when I'd be sitting out there with Joe, he'd get me to talk," Coe recounted. "We'd get to arguing, and he'd say something like: 'What would you do if the company did this, or took over this?' And I'd raise hell about the company, calling them this and calling them that. And he'd say: 'That's not right. You've got class hatred. You shouldn't have that, if you want to be unionized. You've got to have class consciousness.'"

Others remembered the veteran miner rowing kids across the lake while teaching them the words to the famous Socialist anthem, "The Red Flag" ("Though cowards flinch and traitors sneer/We'll keep the red flag flying here.").

Joe Naylor died of cancer in 1946. During his final days, friends sat in shifts at the Cumberland Hospital to keep him company until he breathed his last. He was laid to rest in the Cumberland cemetery, close to his friend Ginger Goodwin. At the gravesite, local UMWA president J.H. Cameron provided a brief resumé of Naylor's life, paying tribute to his long, unwavering commitment to the labour movement. As mourners bowed their heads, local union secretary John Bond read out the UMWA burial commemoration from their 1912 constitution: "We are assembled here today to pay a last sad tribute of love to our departed friend and brother . . . and now we pay the last rite . . . placing on your grave these evergreens, as a token of respect, that thy memory shall be with us always, though thou hath paid the debt and hast gone to the realms above."

SOURCES

My thanks to Donna Sacuta and Patricia Wejr of the BC Labour Heritage Centre for their invaluable assistance in researching Joe Naylor.

FOLVIK, ROBIN, DALE M. MCCARTNEY, AND MARK LEIER. *Pray for the Dead, But Fight Like Hell for the Living: An Introduction to Ginger Goodwin, Joseph Naylor, Lucy Parsons and Mother Jones.* N.p.: BCGEU, n.d. https://yusapuy.ca/wp-content/uploads/2019/11/Mark-Leier-CCU-Feb-2019-Pray-for-the-Dead-Fight-for-the-Living.pdf

ISSIT, BENJAMIN. "Searching for Workers' Solidarity: The One Big Union and the Victoria General Strike of 1919." *Labour/Le Travail* 60 (Fall 2007): 9-42. https://www.lltjournal.ca/index.php/llt/article/view/5507

MAYSE, SUSAN. *Ginger: The Life and Death of Albert Goodwin.* Madeira Park, BC: Harbour Publishing, 1990.

MCCARTNEY, DALE MICHAEL. "A Crisis of Commitment: Socialist Internationalism in British Columbia during the Great War." Thesis submitted in partial fulfillment for a Master of Arts degree. Simon Fraser University, 2010. https://summit.sfu.ca/item/9970

MICKLEBURGH, ROD. "Joe Naylor." Produced by the BC Labour Heritage Centre. *On the Line: Stories of BC Workers.* Episode 1, n.d. Podcast. https://www.labourheritagecentre.ca/podcast/

MICKLEBURGH, ROD. *On the Line: A History of the British Columbia Labour Movement.* Madeira Park, BC: Harbour Publishing, 2018.

MINERS MEMORIAL WEEKEND. "*Canadian Mineworker.* 'Joe Naylor, Staunch Trade Unionist Dies.' 1946." Facebook, October 5, 2018. https://www.facebook.com/MinersMemorialCumberland/photos/a.300263107097746/562571140866940/?type=3

STONEBANKS, ROGER. *Fighting for Dignity: The Ginger Goodwin Story*. St John's: Canadian Committee on Labour History, 2004. https://www.aupress.ca/books/cclh16-fighting-for-dignity/

STONEBANKS, ROGER. "Joe Naylor: Man of Principle." *Times Colonist*, September 21, 1997, Sunday Island Reader. https://www.labourheritagecentre.ca/wordpress/wp-content/uploads/2017/07/Joe-Naylor-Stonebank.pdf

WINSTANLEY, DEREK AND RAY WINSTANLEY. *Founded on Coal: A History of a Coal Mining Community: The Parish of St. Matthew Highfield and Winstanley*. Winstanley, UK: R. Winstanley, 1981.

5

Springing the Trap

The Tale of the Flying Dutchman

DAVE FLAWSE

Stooped in the coved entryway of the Fraser and Bishop General Store in Union Bay, a man yanks a skeleton key from his pocket. He gropes for the door's lock and shoves the key in. The door groans open. Cloaked in midnight's shadows, he and a second man slink inside, their footfalls deadened by soft-soled shoes. Once more, the man sinks a hand deep into the pocket of his Mackinaw coat. With a wink of his electric flashlight, he exposes the unguarded loot. Before the men can stuff their sacks, a lock jiggles at the store's second entrance and the two freeze. The first man again thrusts a hand into his coat. This time he wrenches out a .44 calibre Colt revolver. Their hearts thump. They crouch between counters filled with dried goods and breathe air choked with spices and sweat. The man aims the Colt at the second entrance.

What happened next? For over a century, various writers have recounted the story of one of Vancouver Island's most infamous shootouts. From the first time I read about the notorious pirate and smuggler nicknamed the Flying Dutchman and his exploits in Union Bay, I wanted to write my own version of the tale. I began my research by scouring the handful of published versions out there. But I noticed inconsistencies between them. Unsure of which ones to believe, I quested for the truth. The source documents I unearthed from both Canadian and American archives, prison records, and newspapers not only illuminated the small details but also called into question whether the gunman deserved his final judgment: execution.

IN 1870, OVER FORTY YEARS before the general store robbery at Union Bay, one of Louisiana's newest residents was a squalling baby named Henry Ferguson Sastro. The baby looked up at his German-born parents through steel-grey eyes. Other distinguishing features included a mole on his right cheek and bow legs that never straightened out. In 1882, his father died, followed six years later by his mother. Eighteen years old and parentless, Sastro possessed a face that looked as if it could take a punch. Standing 173 centimetres (5 feet 8 inches) tall and weighing in at eighty-two kilograms (180 pounds) of muscle and bone, no doubt he could deliver punches too. At some point he joined the U.S. Merchant Marines, a civilian organization responsible for international and domestic seaborne trade. Here he became steeped in the life of a seaman.

A DECADE BEFORE THE ROBBERY, on October 18, 1901, two police officers scrambled from their boat at a Whidbey Island dock in Puget Sound. The officers rushed a nearby cabin and flung the door open, guns drawn. Inside, Sastro and another man raised their hands. The officers charged Sastro with the theft of thirty-five sacks of oats from a warehouse a year earlier. Long since a Scotsman's breakfast, the oats were a minor, easy-to-prove offence.

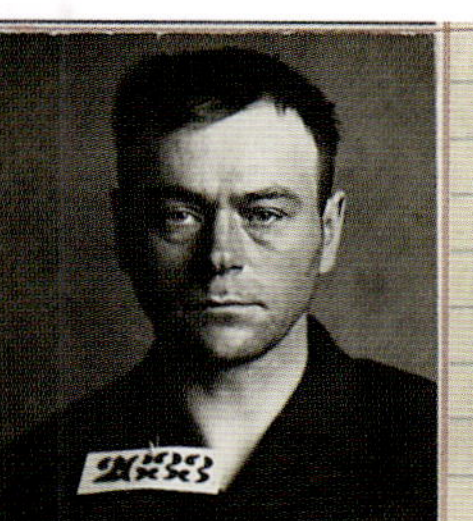

No. 2633 Name Henry Ferguson
Alias H. F. Saster
Crime Burglary
Age 31 Height 5'8" Weight
Build Hair Brown Eyes Blue
Comp. Born La.
Occupation Mechanic Nativity German
Rec'd from Snohomish Co Sentence 14 Yrs.
12/23/01

Marks and Scars
3 Dim vac marks on each upper arm.
Mole on right cheek.
Dim scar over right eyebrow.

Remarks
Discharged
8/1/08

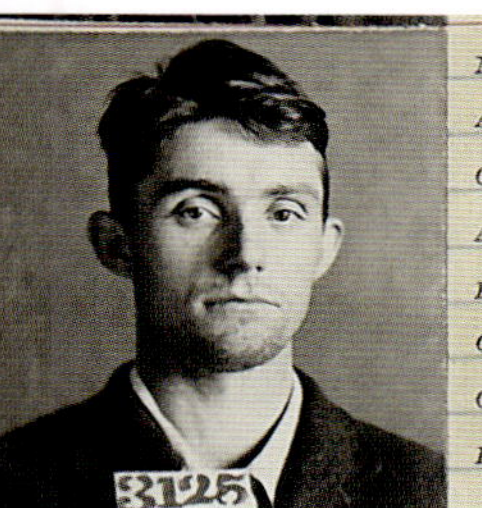

No. 3125 Name Wm. JULIAN
Alias
Crime Grand Larceny
Age 32 Height 5'3¼" Weight
Build Hair Brown Eyes Brown
Comp. Born Wales
Occupation Laborer Nativity English
Rec'd from Snohomish Co Sentence 3 Yrs.
7/17/03

Marks and Scars
Vac mark on left upper arm.
Cut scar near center forehead.
Cut scar ½" above right eyebrow.

Remarks
Discharged
10/26/05

TOP Mugshot of Henry Ferguson, aka Henry Wagner or "The Flying Dutchman," arrested in Washington State for burglary in 1901. WASHINGTON STATE ARCHIVES, AR129-5-8-PH002632.

MIDDLE Mugshot of William Julian, arrested in Washington State for grand larceny in 1903. WASHINGTON STATE ARCHIVES, AR129-5-8-PH003124.

In court two months later, Sastro admitted to a more wicked crime: smuggling nine thousand pounds of opium from Canada to the United States over a number of years. The judge sentenced him to fourteen years of hard labour at Walla Walla State Penitentiary.

The penitentiary was a prisoner-run, self-contained city that produced goods for sale—like grain sacks for oats. Inside, Sastro met the man who would eventually become the number one witness in his murder trial. In 1903, William Julian got three years hard time for grand larceny. Of Welsh heritage, Julian was born in the same era as Sastro. His lustrous black hair sat atop a baby face with a Celtic complexion. In contrast to Sastro, the slender man stood at 5 feet 3 inches and weighed 135 pounds.

Sastro was released in 1908 for good behaviour, but that behaviour failed to extend beyond incarceration. In 1909, a "Wanted" poster pegged Henry Ferguson (by now he had dropped Sastro from his name) as the prime suspect in a post office robbery in Washington State. He and two other men had snuck in at night and stolen $176.80. A self-taught locksmith, Ferguson

BURGLARY

Wanted for Postoffice, Store and Launch Burglary.

The Postoffice at Langley, on Whidby Island, Wash., across from Everett, was robbed on the night of July 15, 1909, and the safe looted of $176.80. Admission was gained with skeleton key and combination of the safe worked or had not been locked.

The burglary was committed by Henry Ferguson, John McDonald and Nels J. Jorgenson. McDonald and Jorgensen were captured. Ferguson is still at large.

Water Pirate Henry Ferguson; alias "Jack the Flying Dutchman" whose description is as follows: Age 39; heighth 5 feet 10 inches; hair dark and may be a little gray; eyes steel gray; medium complexion; weiggt about 180 pounds; a little bow legged, and is a little stooped. Water pirate; wears black cap when in boat and light-colored canvass hat when on shore. Is generally armed with a 44-calibre Colt's revolver and carries it in his right hip pocket, and a double-barreled shot-gun with 17-inch barrels. He has a 16-ft. long, square and copper painted boat with small deck forward and apt, 3 horse power gasoline engine, Phirro make, small sail, no cabin when last seen, but may have repainted the boat. Ferguson is probably accompanied by a man by the name of Wm Julian, described as follows: height about 5 ft. 5½ in. dark hair; eyes brown; complexion dark; about 36 years old, and a half-breed Indian woman, all of whom are supposed to be in Nanaimo, B. C., or vicinity, as their plan was to rob a company store at that place. Both of these men are desperate characters, and I am informed left here about a week ago for B. C. for the purpose of murdering two men and committing a robbery.

Ferguson is well posted on the B. C. waters and on Puget Sound. He talks about Yulu Island, Frazer river and Bring Berge Island.

Ferguson is an ex-convict and is wanted in Island county for burglary, and his capture is of the utmost importance on account of the crimes he has committed and for those he threatens to commit.

I am very anxious to get this man and will appreciate any information which may lead to his arrest.

Wire any information at my expense.

MARKUS WANGSNESS,
Sheriff of Island County.
Coupeville, Washington.

ABOVE A 1909 "Wanted" poster highlights Ferguson's criminal past and suggests he's planning to rob a store in the Nanaimo area. WASHINGTON STATE ARCHIVES, WSP 2633 FERGUSON.

gained entry with a skeleton key and worked a safe. Police captured the other two culprits, but "Water Pirate Henry Ferguson, alias 'Jack the Flying Dutchman,'" escaped. The alias Flying Dutchman comes from sailors' tales of a ghost ship that has haunted the seas for centuries. Sighting the ship foretells doom. The people of North America's Pacific Coast affixed the name to Ferguson somewhere along his travels.

The poster explained that he "wears a black cap when in boat and a light-coloured canvas hat when on shore" and "is generally armed with a Colt .44 revolver and a double-barreled shotgun." Known to be handy and clever, Ferguson would sometimes repaint and refit the cabin on his 16-foot boat, the *Spray*. With a three-horsepower gasoline engine and small sail, the *Spray* was quick and nimble.

The poster referenced Ferguson, William Julian, and a woman of mixed Indigenous ancestry, "all of whom are supposed to be in Nanaimo, BC, or vicinity, as their plan was to rob a company store at that place. Both of these men are desperate characters, and I am informed left here about a week ago for B.C. for the purpose of murdering two men and committing a robbery." The poster said that "Ferguson is well posted in the B.C. waters and on Puget Sound. He talks about Yulu Island, Frazer River, and Bring Berge Island" (a misspelling and likely reference to Lulu Island—one of the seventeen islands that make up modern-day Richmond—the Fraser River, and Bainbridge Island, west of Seattle). For the Washington authorities, his capture was "of the utmost importance on account of the crimes he has committed and for those he threatens to commit."

This heat is perhaps what drove Ferguson and Julian into Canada, where U.S. law enforcement could not follow. But BC was no safe haven. They had jumped from a sinking ship into a heaving sea. Their Wanted poster trailed the pirates north into Canada, where a man hardened by decades of policing on the coast readied himself.

CHIEF CONSTABLE DAVID STEPHENSON began his job in 1881 as the Island's lone BC Provincial Police officer, stationed north of Esquimalt. Before immigrating to Canada, he had been a member of Queen Victoria's Guard of Honour. He looked every part the Canadian frontier cop—a smart uniform, stabbing glare, and thick, drooping moustache on an otherwise clean-shaven face. In the early days, he travelled the coast alone by canoe to take prisoners to court in Nanaimo. Whether they helped paddle is unknown.

In the years after the Wanted poster's publication, pirates marauded the BC coast, committing a string of burglaries. On October 12, 1912, the *Daily Colonist* reported that thieves blew a safe in Victoria and made away with nearly six hundred dollars. Vancouver saw safe-breaking attempts in the same month. On December 15, burglars broke into the safe at Nanaimo City Hall. Up Island in Union Bay, around the same time, a woman named Mrs. Bishop was working in a hotel kitchen. She heard a noise and went down the hall to investigate. According to *The Friendly Port*, a book about Union Bay's history, a burglar was breaking in and heard her coming. The burglar ducked into a bedroom and hid in a wardrobe. She never did find him, but "Mrs. Bishop's brother was up staying, and he had an old pair of comfortable pants. One day he went to put them on, and they weren't there." Police found the pants months later at the Flying Dutchman's hideout.

With an area eight times larger than Puget Sound under his care and few officers to help him, Stephenson had found it impossible to apprehend the culprits. He needed a break in the case. Convinced the pirates would hit Union Bay again soon, he planned a trap. For this he enlisted two undercover officers. The first, Gordon Ross, had fought in the South African war as a Lovat Scout. The Scottish sniper regiment was famous for being a pioneer of the ghillie suit, a type of camouflage that helped wearers blend in with their background. The second, Harry Westaway, hailed from PEI. Up until his thirtieth birthday he lived with his parents. According to the census, he worked as a painter before becoming an officer. Stephenson posted the two men in Union Bay at the beginning of February 1913.

On March 3, 1913, the Farmers Institute on Lasqueti Island was holding a meeting. Two reputable Lasqueti community members, Henry Wagner and William Julian, told their neighbour in Scottie Bay they were leaving to attend the meeting. At four in the afternoon, Wagner's wife and children watched them motor out of the bay. The next time they saw Wagner, he would be behind bars.

The Flying Dutchman's true name depended on who you asked and where you asked them. The desperado's actions necessitated aliases to elude the authorities. In Washington State, he answered to Henry Ferguson Sastro and Henry Ferguson; on the Canadian side of the line, Henry Wagner.

With his three-horsepower engine, Wagner could travel a little faster than a horse could walk. He never intended to make the Farmers Institute meeting. From Scottie Bay, the most direct route to Union Bay led him west to Hornby Island. Here, he hooked slightly south around Denman Island. One of the few nighttime guides, the blinking Chrome Island lighthouse, lay to starboard just offshore from Denman's southern end. Darkness shrouded the headlands and shoals as they sputtered northwards.

During Wagner and Julian's northbound journey up Baynes Sound, Constables Gordon Ross and Harry Westaway played cards and drank beers in the Nelson Hotel. As the port for the Cumberland coal mines, Union Bay's long wharf welcomed ships from all over the world. A short stroll away, the hotel faced the sea.

ABOVE This 1913 photo of the Fraser and Bishop Store in Union Bay shows glass panes that were broken during a robbery committed by Ferguson and Julian. COURTESY OF LIBRARY & ARCHIVES CANADA, RG13-B-1, VOLUME 1463, FILE 493 A

Its bar was a fine place to spend the evenings, drinking and chatting to travellers. Ross and Westaway had waited for a month, night in and night out, for criminals to appear at the Fraser and Bishop General Store next door. At night, the white building, with its high false front, sat dark and quiet.

At midnight, the officers noticed a light. They walked into the post office adjoining the store to investigate. Once inside, they heard a creak in the store proper, as if someone had stepped on a floorboard. Westaway clutched a pistol. Ross gripped a flashlight and baton. Unknown to them, Wagner was peering down the sights of his Colt .44.

Union Bay's local police officer was on duty not far away at the colliery dock when he heard someone yelling for help. At the store's entryway, the door's shattered glass crunched under his feet. A shadow beckoned him inside. The officer clicked on his flashlight to behold Gordon Ross standing by the door. Beyond him waited a grisly sight—a captive lay unconscious on the floor, bloodied and beaten to a pulp, and Harry Westaway lay dead in a pool of blood.

Chief Constable David Stephenson happened to be in Cumberland that night, visiting another constable, his son, Albert. They received a call about an incident in Union Bay. A bumpy thirty-minute drive down Royston Road and what is now the Island Highway and the two officers arrived on the scene. Someone poured cold water onto the prisoner. Stephenson identified the barely conscious man as the Flying Dutchman.

Wagner was brought to the Cumberland lockup, where he asked to have a reporter sent to take down his story. He planned to sell the story and give the money to his wife. Permission was not granted.

On March 13, 1913, an officer named George Hannay shepherded Wagner to the Nanaimo Gaol. George Hannay and the entire force had had a busy March. They had scoured the area for an unidentified second man who had escaped from the scene of the burglary. After the botched burglary, Julian had taken the *Spray*'s skiff and started rowing the thirty miles back to Lasqueti Island. On March 7, with two aching arms from three days of rowing, Julian arrived on land, only to find Hannay waiting for him, pistol drawn. Perhaps it was Wagner who told police where to find him.

PROCEEDINGS IN WAGNER'S TRIAL began on May 13 at Nanaimo's courthouse. The doctor who arrived on scene early in the morning after the murder testified that Westaway had died from a gunshot wound through his right lung, but was unsure from which direction the bullet had entered. A bullet's exit wound is typically much larger than the entry wound. However, Westaway's two deadly holes measured about the same. As well, the doctor found two gashes about two inches long on the top of Westaway's head. He also noted how Wagner had taken a thrashing while Ross had no marks on him.

Gordon Ross came to the stand next. His testimony went like this: He and Westaway entered the post office and heard the creaking floorboard in the store. Ross pointed his flashlight into the store but saw nothing until he directed the beam to his left, where he found himself looking down the barrel of Wagner's Colt .44. Wagner was crouched on one knee in a narrow corridor between the counters. Ross killed his light and rushed him. Wagner fired. The bullets missed Ross in this narrow corridor and hit Westaway, who was behind him. Westaway said, "I'm shot, Gordon, do you have him?" While Westaway bled out on the floor, Ross and Wagner fought for the gun, knocking supplies off the shelves. The crime scene photos show disarray. Eventually, Ross subdued Wagner, knocked him unconscious, and handcuffed him. Ross admitted during questioning to being punched several times by Wagner.

As the doctor noted, however, Ross was unscathed. He did not even have marks on his knuckles. Victor Harrison, the lawyer assigned to Wagner, raised this anomaly during cross-examination: "What was he fighting," Harrison asked Ross, "the counter or walls? What was he fighting? You are not marked up. I don't understand you." Ross responded, "I don't understand it myself." Harrison asked Ross if he'd had anything to drink that evening. Ross sketchily admitted he'd spent the entire evening in the hotel bar but that he'd drunk only one beer. Post-trial, Harrison stated in a document that he sent to Ottawa to have the case appealed that Ross was a known drunk.

Another question raised by Harrison was how the bullet had missed Ross in the narrow corridor and hit Westaway, who was behind him. Ross did not know.

Wagner's testimony contrasted with Ross's. He claimed a drunken Ross had accidently shot Westaway while Wagner and Westaway wrestled. This version of events might explain why Westaway had two gashes on his head and Ross was unmarked, and it would also solve the bullet wound puzzle. A bullet entering from the back would add some credence to Wagner's version.

The prosecutor asked Wagner about his past crimes. Was it true he'd been a member of Butch Cassidy's Wild Bunch, the infamous American train-robbing gang? Wagner answered no.

Next, Julian came onto the stand. His story was short and simple. He entered the store behind Wagner, clutching his coattails in the dark. When a light flashed on them, Julian fled, and as he exited the store, he heard two gunshots. If true, the timing of the gunshots supports Ross's version of events. As the number one witness against Wagner, Julian sealed Wagner's fate with his testimony. Julian would be tried shortly afterwards for burglary only, not as an accomplice to murder.

In the Nanaimo courthouse, the judge addressed the court and described his take on the events: Wagner entered the store armed with a pistol to commit burglary. He had that pistol to avoid apprehension, if it came to it, and had long prepared to shoot someone. The jury, apparently split until the final minutes, took four hours to come back with a guilty verdict. Wagner was condemned to death by hanging, with his execution set for August 28 of that year.

ABOVE Photos from inside the store show the damage caused by the struggle that took place during the robbery. COURTESY OF LIBRARY & ARCHIVES CANADA, RG13-B-1, VOLUME 1463, FILE 493 A

The case was murky and evidence scant, but the Flying Dutchman had a reputation. After the trial, in the same petition Wagner's lawyer sent to Ottawa to request an appeal, he claimed some jurors had made up their minds to have Wagner executed before the court case began.

THE FLYING DUTCHMAN'S final months were not without drama, both in his cell and on Vancouver Island. Days before the trial, the Island's coal towns erupted in riots. Coal miners demanded better working conditions and threatened to unionize. The situation

ABOVE Photos from inside the store show the damage caused by the struggle that took place during the robbery. COURTESY OF LIBRARY & ARCHIVES CANADA, RG13-B-1, VOLUME 1463, FILE 493 A

prompted the Provincial Police to call in the militia, who made mass arrests. The prisoner records for the Nanaimo Gaol at this time are choked with miners' names.

Beginning the day after the trial, guards watched Wagner around the clock. This was called a death watch. Unlike at Walla Walla, he was assigned no labour, hard or otherwise. In the months leading up to the execution, Mrs. Wagner and the children visited nearly every week. On one visit he gave her $250 from the sale of the *Spray*. She also took his watch, chain, and other effects. The remaining $50 from the $300 boat sale he kept. As with the gaols in Victoria and New Westminster at the time, prisoners condemned to death could purchase and cook their own food. Wagner regularly bought eggs, butter, and bacon, which the guards delivered to him.

After a final visit from his wife and children, Wagner attempted suicide by banging his head against the radiator in the shower. After that, guards shackled his legs with a chain so short he could only shuffle his feet.

ARTHUR ELLIS, the Dominion of Canada's official executioner, had hanged hundreds. Ellis was only the latest of many forefathers to undertake this grim task. Untold numbers met their end by his kin, who had been executing people for over three hundred years. The night before his current task, Ellis stepped into Wagner's cell. He placed two fingers on the prisoner's wrist—a touch to measure a pulse by the man who would steal it.

Due to the miners' strikes, the execution was closed to the public. In the early morning of August 28, 1913, a handful of police constables, a Salvation Army officer, and Ellis gathered in Nanaimo's gaol courtyard. Silence filled the dewy air. The assembled men faced the wooden gallows, where a noose, rigid and still, hung from the top beam. At the platform's crest, high above the witnesses, the executioner grasped a black sack and leather straps. A door to the courtyard flew open. The Flying Dutchman stumbled into the sunlight.

The hanging began at 7:45 a.m. in the gaol's courtyard. According to a first-hand account of the execution published in *Outlaws and Lawmen of Western Canada*, the conditions were right for Ellis to attempt a world record for the fastest hanging. Ellis had noted that the distance between the courtyard door and the gallows in Nanaimo matched the location in England where the current record was set by his uncle. He left the bottom of the gallows unscreened so the timekeeper could see the moment the condemned man's toes hit the gravel.

WHEN WAGNER STUMBLES into the courtyard, those gathered lift their hats, not out of respect for the convicted murderer but because it is the law. As soon as Wagner reaches the trap on the gallows, Ellis yanks the sack over his head, pinions his legs with the strap, and jerks the noose tight behind his ears. Before the Salvation Army officer can say four words of the Lord's Prayer, Ellis springs the trap. The Flying Dutchman's third vertebra snaps, his toes graze the gravel below the scaffolding, and he meets Death instantly.

Ellis thrusts his hand into the air. "Time!"

PUBLISHED VERSIONS OF THIS STORY have invariably painted the Flying Dutchman as a cold-hearted desperado and the police as heroes. This is a common narrative in any story where a police officer is murdered, but truth is rarely so cut and dried. The BC Provincial Police both protected and acted against the public. According to volume three of *British Columbia: From the Past Times to the Present*, a biographical account of prominent community members, Chief Constable David Stephenson was respected and generally considered a fair officer. Conversely, a common photo of Stephenson shows him leading a gang of mounted constables, ready to quell the strikes in Nanaimo.

In the case of the Flying Dutchman, Stephenson managed to stop the crime spree, but one of his officers paid for the victory with his life. What Stephenson thought of the justice Wagner received, we don't know. Other problems were likely at the forefront of his mind. The strikes continued, only abating during the First World War. In 1916, Stephenson retired at his own request after thirty-six years on duty. After the war ended, the strikes worsened.

Other BC Provincial Police constables were indistinguishable from the criminals they arrested. Not long after the Flying Dutchman was hanged, William Julian pled guilty to breaking into the Fraser and Bishop General Store and served a five-year sentence. Shortly after his release, police scoured the coast for two pirates who were robbing communities in the same manner Wagner and Julian had. Police caught up to Julian on February 18, 1920, and arrested him. The next day they arrested his accomplice: George Hannay, the officer who had arrested Julian on Lasqueti Island in 1913.

SOURCES

ANACORTES AMERICAN. "Washington News." November 21, 1901. https://washingtondigitalnewspapers.org/?a=D&D=ANACAMER19011121.2.64&srpos=1&e=01-1-1900-01-12-1902--en-20--1--txt-txIN-%22henry+ferguson%22------

BC ARCHIVES. Nanaimo Gaol Records. GR-0310 Vol. 1–20.

DAILY COLONIST. "Safeblowers Get Booty in Laundry." October 6, 1912. https://archive.org/details/dailycolonist57253uvic/page/n9/mode/1up?view=theateR&Q=burglar

DAILY COLONIST. "Attempt to Crack Safe." October 9, 1912. https://archive.org/details/dailycolonist57255uvic/mode/1up?view=theateR&Q=burglars

DAILY COLONIST. "Burglars." December 15, 1912. https://archive.org/details/dailycolonist57313uvic/page/n22/mode/1up?view=theateR&Q=burglars

DOWNS, ART, ED. *Outlaws and Lawmen of Western Canada*, Vol. II. Victoria, BC: Heritage House Publishing, 1983.

GEIDT, JANETTE GLOVER. *The Friendly Port: A History of Union Bay 1880–1960*. Union Bay, BC: D. R. Geidt, 1990.

LIBRARY AND ARCHIVES CANADA. RG 13, vol. 1463, file 493A; 1913.

MASON, ELDA COPLEY. *Lasqueti Island History and Memory*. Self-published, 1976.

SCHOLEFIELD, E. O. S. *British Columbia: From the Past Times to the Present*, Vol. III. Vancouver: The S. J. Clarke Publishing Company, 1914.

SEATTLE STAR. "Surprised, Sound Pirate and Pal, and Captured 'Em." October 15, 1901. Washington State Archives WSP 2633 Ferguson. https://washingtondigitalnewspapers.org/?a=D&D=SEATSTAR19011015.1.4&srpos=3&e=01-1-1900-01-12-1902--en-20--1--txt-txIN-%22henry+ferguson%22------

6

One Stout-Hearted Entrepreneur

BEVIN CLEMPSON

The laughter of PE'ntlatc (Pentlatch) children on the shore of Metcalf Bay, British Columbia, is carried along by the soft wind. In the early morning light, silhouettes of their parents at work harvesting clams and oysters dot the shoreline. The air is already heavy with warmth. The oars dip in and out of the glassy water, and the boat, loaded with fruit, meat, vegetables, and children, moves swiftly across the narrow strait. The woman pauses to wipe beads of sweat from her brow and then continues rowing as they slip around the point toward Fanny Bay.

The row across Baynes Sound takes anywhere from forty-five to sixty minutes. Upon docking, they continue the trip by horse and cart. The year is 1889, and Diana Pickard Day Piket has sixteen hungry lodgers to feed, along with five children aged twelve and under. While her husband, John Henry Piket, farms their property on Denman Island, Diana provides wholesome meals and accommodation to miners working in the newly established coal mines in Union Camp—fifteen miles away.

In the late nineteenth and early twentieth centuries, the coal-mining towns that dotted Vancouver Island's rugged landscape were notoriously gritty. They were isolated, company-owned communities with sizable populations of migratory male workers lacking formal housing and basic amenities. Union was no different. Located halfway up the east coast of Vancouver Island, the community was, literally and figuratively, built on coal.

Rich deposits were first discovered in the area in 1852. A group of prospectors quickly took advantage of the provincial government's offer of land for investment in coal development and established the Union Coal Company in 1869. Mines were developed in the 1870s, but funds ran low, and the company was sold to the Dunsmuir family in 1883 to become part of the Union Colliery Company (UCC). The first mine in the area opened in 1888, with seven more to follow, and the settlement saw a frenzied period of growth well into the 1890s. By 1891, considerable amounts of domestic coal were coming from the pits and being sent to the docks at Union Bay for shipment around the world. In June of 1891, the mines closed due to a lack of coal sales in San Francisco. Development slowed, and most men were let go and moved elsewhere to find work. Five months later, production resumed and enthusiastic expansion of the town continued.

With the Dunsmuir family promising steady wages and a prosperous life in Canada, able-bodied workers arrived from all over the world—Australia, Chile, China, England, Ireland, Italy, Japan, Norway, Scotland, and Sweden—creating pockets of mini communities divided by ethnicity within the camp. As the population increased, the number of buildings exploded beyond the hundred or so that made up the original mining settlement, and the town soon reached its geographical limitations. James Dunsmuir designated one hundred acres east of Union as the area for a new town. A plan was drafted, blocks and lots were surveyed, and the townsite was designated as Cumberland in 1893. It is unclear who gets credit for choosing Cumberland as the name for the town, but there is consensus that it was chosen in honour of miners who arrived from the mining county of Cumberland on England's northwest coast, which shares a border with Scotland to the north. Many of Cumberland's streets are named after places in the county of Cumberland.

Development was fast. Single-family homes and boarding houses were built. By the time it was incorporated in 1897, Cumberland had several churches, a jailhouse, a courthouse, an eight-room school, ample entertainment venues including hotels, and a recorded population of three thousand. While mine workers and their families made up a good portion of the population, various entrepreneurs saw economic potential in the townsite and capitalized on its growth—offering much-needed products and services such as barbers, dry goods, drugs and sundries, hardware, hotels, liquor, fresh produce, and more. Women were among the entrepreneurs setting up shop, and Diana Piket was well ahead of the rest.

In 1876, at the age of nineteen, Diana Pickard Day married John Henry Piket, aged twenty, in Nottingham, England. Seven years later, they immigrated to Canada with two young children, Nellie (six) and Thomas (four). The young couple grew vegetables and raised livestock on their land on Denman Island and continued growing their family. A second son, Leonard, was born in 1885. He was the first of their children to be born in Canada and is thought to be the first white child born on Denman Island. Two daughters soon followed, Mahala in 1887 and Carrie in 1892.

Rows of green leaves emerge from the damp soil, and small white flowers have begun to appear; on the trees, summer apples have started to show their colour. The two oldest girls collect eggs from the dozen hens—the rustle of feathers can be heard from the pasture, where the boys are helping their father mend fences. The youngest daughter sits at her mother's feet, splashing tiny fingers about the wash tub. A soft humming can be heard over the sound of scrubbing.

While John Henry continued to farm their land on Denman, Diana ran the largest boarding house in Union for five years. Equipped with a strong sense of discipline and her own brand of care and affection, she took in single miners and other labourers. Diana and John Henry saw a business opportunity in the new

ABOVE The Cumberland Hotel, c. 1894. Diana Piket and her husband bought the hotel three months after it opened in early 1894 and soon built an adjoining hall. Diana ran the hotel until 1905, when she sold it. CUMBERLAND MUSEUM & ARCHIVES COLLECTION, C030-324

townsite of Cumberland and announced they would build a hotel there. Instead, they purchased the newly constructed three-storey Cumberland Hotel, which had opened its doors on New Year's Day of 1894. Three months after its opening, owners John "Jack" Bruce and George Grant McDonald sold the establishment to the Pikets.

Located on the corner of Dunsmuir Avenue and Second Street, it was the first hotel in Cumberland. It soon became one of the main places to go for a drink, play billiards, or conduct business. Almost immediately, the Pikets built a public hall next to the hotel and used it to host large social events—many of which were organized by Diana, an avid entertainer, active philanthropist, and faithful community builder.

The scents of cigars, liquor, and perfume mix in the cool evening air. Piano chords grow louder as the door opens, and hearty laughter spills out. A man staggers, his boots thumping along the dry, wooden sidewalk as he slowly makes his way to the next drink. Next door, quiet falls across the room as smartly dressed men and women take their assigned seats. The hostess has announced that the dinner they generously purchased is about to be served. Conversation continues as drinks are poured and plates are filled with roast beef, turnip, carrots, potatoes, and gravy.

Well known for her catering and entertaining, Diana spent much of her time organizing fundraisers, teas, and other events for community groups like the Red Cross, Cumberland General Hospital Ladies Auxiliary, Harmony Rebekah Lodge, and Holy Trinity Anglican Church. In 1906, she hosted a lovely luncheon for Governor General Earl Grey that was attended by the newly appointed Lieutenant-Governor James Dunsmuir (son of Robert Dunsmuir and owner of the UCC).

After twenty years of marriage, Mr. and Mrs. John Henry Piket went their separate ways in 1896. John Henry purchased the Spring Inn, located between the towns of Cumberland and Courtenay, and renamed it Halfway House. Rumours flew that it was a brothel and den of sins. Diana remained steadfast as one of the few women in business in the area. She kept on as the proprietress of the Cumberland Hotel, bringing in John "Jack" Bruce, one of the original owners, as her partner. Jack promptly moved into the hotel and got to work operating the hotel bar. During Diana's ownership, the Cumberland Hotel was praised as first-class accommodation for permanent and transient boarders. It was also known as a reputable place for businessmen and professionals to have offices and showrooms until they were able to establish themselves elsewhere.

In 1909, after fifteen years in the hotel business, Diana bought a house and leased the Cumberland Hotel and Pikets' Hall to William and Rosalie Merrifield before selling it to them and William's brother, George, in 1912. The house she purchased had been constructed in 1895 at 3312 Fifth Street, just beyond Cumberland's town limits, for newlyweds Frank and Josie Smith. Rather stately at the time, it boasted several windows, a gabled roof, and two floors with a second-floor veranda. The home was rented out in 1897 and is thought to have been used as a guest house for the colliery from 1898 until being sold in 1908, and then sold again, to Diana, in 1909. After moving in, Diana named her home Belvoir Villa, perhaps after Castle Belvoir in Leicestershire, England, close to where she was born and lived with her father, mother, and seven older siblings until her marriage to John Henry. Today the house is commonly known as the Twisted Chimney.

Diana lived in the house for sixteen years, taking in boarders and holding impressive garden parties that raised money for several causes. In 1925, nearing the age of seventy, Diana downsized and moved next door to 3322 Fifth Street, a little, red house that may have housed servants when Belvoir Villa was used as a guest house. She eventually sold her home in 1929.

Although they lived separate lives, Diana and John Henry never divorced. On January 4, 1914, she became a widow when he died after a bout of pneumonia. By this time, John Henry had lost the Halfway House to debts, and it burned to the ground shortly after his death, with great speculation that an angry mob of women did the job. At this time, death was becoming a little too frequent in Diana's life. Three years earlier, her daughter Mahala passed away. Mahala was twenty-four-years-old and had lost her third child, three-month-old Olive, five days earlier. Left behind were her husband of five years, Joseph Hudson, and a son and a daughter, both of whom were aged under five.

After Diana's separation from John Henry, she and Jack Bruce became more than business partners—they became good friends and developed an intimate relationship. Although Jack was seven years her junior, they shared compassionate views about their community and those who called it home. Jack was a founding member of the Cumberland Volunteer Fire Department (CVFD), serving first as the assistant fire chief and then as fire chief from 1898 until 1911. He was also involved in several fraternal and friendly societies, like the Independent Order of Good Templars (IOGT), arranged and participated in many community celebrations, and competed in various athletic competitions, like shot-put and hammer throws. Jack and Diana married in early December of 1916, with Diana taking Jack's surname. Sadly, Diana was widowed, once again, seven months later. Jack Bruce died on July 14, 1917, at the age of fifty-three. Diana never married again. She died seventeen years later.

Life was not easy for women in Diana Bruce's time, but she lived a full life. She thrived in all the situations in which she found herself, first as a farmer, then as a businesswoman, philanthropist, and mother raising five children in a spirited, hard-working community that grew alongside them. Her children all received an education, and as adults they all married and had children of their own. By 1917, Diana was the grandmother of fifteen grandchildren, many of whom lived close by.

After nearly eighty years, Diana's life came to an end on January 2, 1934. Predeceased by her parents, all seven siblings, two husbands, one child, and a granddaughter, Diana rests peacefully between her husbands in the Cumberland Cemetery—in the company of generations of people who helped shape the culture and community of Cumberland. Just as she did.

SOURCES

ANCESTRY.COM. *1871 England Census* [database online]. Lehi, UT, USA: Ancestry.com Operations Inc., 2004.

ANCESTRY.COM. *British Columbia, Canada, Marriage Index, 1872-1935* [database online]. Provo, UT, USA: Ancestry.com Operations Inc., 2001.

ANCESTRY.COM. *Diana (Dinah) Pickard Day, Wetherell Family Tree* [database online]. Provo, UT, USA: Ancestry.com Operations Inc., 2023.

ANCESTRY.COM. *Nottinghamshire, England, Church of England Marriages and Banns, 1754-1937* [database online]. Lehi, UT, USA: Ancestry.com Operations, Inc., 2022.

CAIRNS, BRETT. *History of the Comox Valley*. Self-published, 2017.

COOK, DENISE AND ELANA ZYSBLAT. "Village of Cumberland Statement of Significance - Camp Road." The Village of Cumberland, 2018. https://cumberland.ca/wp-content/uploads/2018/09/HC-Agenda-Package-10-Sept-2018.pdf

MOFFORD, GLEN A. *Along the E&N: A Journey Back to the Historic Hotels of Vancouver Island*. Victoria, BC: TouchWood Editions, 2019.

NELL BARR, JENNIFER. *Cumberland Heritage: A Selected History of People, Buildings, Institutions and Sites 1888-1950*. Cumberland, BC: Corporation of the Village of Cumberland, 1997.

STEPHENS, E.G., D.E. WATSON, AND D.E. ISENOR. *One Hundred Spirited Years: A History of Cumberland 1888-1988*. Campbell River, BC: Ptarmigan Press, 1988.

"UP THE LAKE." Cumberland Museum & Archives (blog), August 18, 2020. https://cumberlandmuseum.ca/up-the-lake

VILLAGE OF CUMBERLAND. "History of Cumberland." Updated November 28, 2023.https://cumberland.ca/history

7

Cumberland Chinatown

My Hometown

DR. TOM L.Q. WONG

My childhood in Cumberland's Chinatown was happy. I had family and friends, my family had enough to eat, and we felt safe. Despite poverty, prejudice, and the early loss of my father, we not only survived but ultimately thrived.

The people of Cumberland's Chinatown, a community loathed and marginalized by the dominant society of the time, created a place of belonging, acceptance, and joy. Friendships grew into deep kinship between unrelated families. Cumberland's Chinatown is not a hometown fixed to a place in the distant past that no longer exists but rather a hometown that lives on in our hearts. Former residents are connected by shared memories of relationships that shaped not only who we would become but also the generations that followed us.

Our Home in Cumberland

I was born in 1930 in our family's home in Chinatown. Our neighbour and midwife, Mrs. Wong, who was married to the town's herbalist, delivered me. My family lived upstairs in a building that housed my dad's store on the ground floor. Six of us kids slept in two bedrooms. The two youngest, Jerry and Fanny (who was born two months after our father died), slept in Mom's room, and the rest of us shared a room. Lilly had her own bed, and Lila, Benny, and I shared the other bed, with Lila at one end of the bed and us boys at the other.

A lot of Chinese people were used to sleeping on a wooden board supported by feet much like those of a sawhorse and covered with straw mats, blankets, or comforters. They would rest their heads on wooden pillows.

We had mattresses on our bed, and we were regularly bitten by bed bugs until we got rid of them by getting up in the middle of the night with our flashlights after their bellies were full. They congregated in the seams of the mattresses, and there we crushed them with our fingernails, which produced a distinctive stench. We then soaked the seams of the mattresses with kerosene and this seemed to keep them away for good.

We had electricity and cold running water. An outhouse was attached to the end of our house, but if we had to empty our bladders in the middle of the night, we would use chamber pots. Before we took a bath in the galvanized tub every other week, we would heat up the water on the wood-burning stove. The rest of the time, we just sponge-bathed with warm water.

Most families in Chinatown warmed their homes by burning wood or coal. Our family would buy two tons of coal to heat the house for a full year. We had no refrigeration. Perishable food would be stored on the shady side of the house in two wooden boxes with screens on the side to keep the bugs out and a hinged door in the front. When we bought meat from the butcher, it came unwrapped on a thin, flat bamboo skewer. We would carry the meat home by holding onto a loop at one end of the skewer and hang it up using the same loop. Meat might last just a day or two without spoiling.

Cumberland's Chinatown

At its peak in the 1920s, the population of Cumberland's Chinatown was between 1,200 and 1,500 people. Most of the Chinese men had immigrated to Canada to work in the coal mines with the hope of earning enough money to support their families back in China and then bring them to Canada. Their willingness to work in dangerous conditions for low wages was attractive for the owners of the coal mine, but the racism of the times would destroy the men's dreams.

In 1923, after explosions in the coal mines were blamed on the Chinese, neither Chinese nor Japanese workers were allowed to work underground. Chinese men were allowed to maintain the railway tracks and to load coal onto the ships in Union Bay. The *Chinese Immigration Act* (*Chinese Exclusion Act*), which was passed in 1923, blocked the further immigration of Chinese people into Canada.

The Chinatown of my childhood had only six or seven families living in a forsaken area in a swampy valley on the side of a mountain, but in addition to these few families, hundreds of men lived there alone. The men who lived alone—some had families back in China and some were single, with little prospect of finding a wife after the *Chinese Exclusion Act* came into effect—would informally adopt or be adopted by a family. They would join the family for special meals at Easter or Christmastime, bringing treats like bread and butter, cakes, or cookies.

After my father died, these men befriended me and were very helpful, doing repairs and maintenance in our home. I learned so much from them. I would often be invited to their homes to enjoy some good meals such as poached chicken or tasty pork chops cooked in cast iron pots and pans.

George Wong was one of those kind and generous friends who adopted my family as his own. He would treat a couple of us kids to a movie when a new one came to town, and if he noticed my shoes were worn down or outgrown, he would take me to the store and buy me a new pair.

One of my happiest summers was spent cutting trees with three family friends, Young Fook, Wong Sun, and Wong Poy. Wong Sun and Wong Poy were contract fallers. Young Fook bucked the logs and trimmed the branches and was skilled at sharpening saws.

The dirt roads of Chinatown were about 130 feet across and would sometimes flood with the rain. The ground floor of our house also frequently flooded. As a teen, I used cedar planks to raise the ground floor by eight inches so that my family would no longer get their feet soaked when they were leaving the house. The sidewalk was a boardwalk, and of course, all the houses were simple wood buildings.

No one in our community owned their house. The properties were all owned by the coal-mining company. No one would pay to live where we lived. In 1936, a great fire burned down many of the Chinatown homes. The blaze began in a newly shingled house where shingles had been used to start a fire for cooking.

My Father's Life in Cumberland and His Early Passing

My father, Why Wong, came to Canada in 1894 and settled in Cumberland during the town's coal-mining heyday. I don't know what his job was with the coal mine. By the time I was born, he was a butcher and a merchant, and his store took up the main floor of our home. He was one of the few Chinese men who owned a truck, and I remember going with him as a preschooler on some of his meat deliveries to the Japanese and Chinese communities.

My dad was tall, slim, and soft-spoken. Because he spent most of his time working, I didn't see much of him except at suppertime. I remember him as a kind and gentle man, but I wish I had

LEFT Dr. Tom Wong's parents, Why Wong (*left*) and Lee Cow, stand with their eldest three children (*left to right*), Benny, Lila, and Lilly, c. 1930. COURTESY OF DR. TOM WONG

had more time with him. I was only five when he died in 1935 at the age of sixty-two.

My poor mom was widowed at twenty-five with six children to care for. Mom had to close the store, though we continued to live in the rooms upstairs.

My Mother's Difficult Life

My mom, Lee Cow, was born in China in 1910, and her life was never easy. At the age of eight, she was sold by her family to the wealthy Yip family as a servant. She was not given an education and never learned to read, write, or speak English, though she was brought by the Yip family to Vancouver in 1918. In 1923, at the age of thirteen, she was sold to my father as his wife. My mother never spoke about her life prior to their marriage.

As a child, I thought at first that my mom was not very smart because she could not read or write, but I soon realized that she was exceptionally intelligent, strong, and resilient. She kept her

six children fed and clothed. She grew vegetables, cooked, crocheted, and knitted, and she did alterations to earn a little money. She found countless ways to help us survive.

Although she was less than four feet ten inches tall, she would do her chores with a baby strapped on her back, and she could carry a hundred-pound sack of rice up the stairs to our kitchen.

ABOVE Why died in 1935 and Lee raised their six children as a single mother. Here she poses with four of them (*left to right*), Lilly, Jerry, Fanny, and Tom (the author), c. 1940. COURTESY OF DR. TOM WONG

Work and Play as a Child in Cumberland

We kids all helped out from a young age. I remember at age eight rolling eighteen-inch blocks of wood with two poles nailed into each end the quarter mile home to be used as firewood, and helping our mom gather the waste from outhouses to use for fertilizer in the garden. After school, we each did our chores. In those days, the Chinese people liked Spam sandwiches but would cut off the crusts and toss them out. One of my jobs was to gather these scraps of bread and feed them to our chickens. Because it was a one-mile walk to town, neighbours would ask me to ride my bike to buy food and other supplies they couldn't get in Chinatown. One man had been enjoying cheap and tasty canned food that he called the Cat brand. When we enquired in town, it turned out that it was cat food.

We would hike with one or two other families up the hills outside of Chinatown to pick blackberries. They were the sweetest berries I have ever tasted, and they made the best jams and pies. Mom would send us door to door to sell them. A ten-pound bucket would sell for one dollar, and at the end of the day, we would be given five cents to buy a Popsicle. My older sisters,

Lilly and Lila, hated selling berries. They inevitably failed to make many sales, and I would be sent out instead. Most of the customers could not resist buying berries from the younger—and cuter—kid.

I had a variety of jobs as a teen. I used to hitch a huge workhorse to haul the mine timbers. Later, I cut the mine timbers, and eventually, I felled trees. I had a casual job shovelling coal onto the ships in Union Bay. I wasn't given a mask or any other protective wear, and by the end of a shift, I would be covered with coal dust. I would ride my bike to Comox Lake and jump in the cool water to wash up before heading home. I remember the shocking sheen of the coal dust covering the surface of the water.

We kids had fun too. As preschoolers, my playmates and I liked to walk to the creek, a quarter mile from home. We would ask one of the older men in town to take us there, and they would keep an eye on us as we took our shoes off, played with the minnows, and built little dams with mud, stones, and sticks. We had many guardians to watch over us in our little town, and we felt safe.

TOP Tom Wong follows his mother over a wooden boardwalk to cut firewood, c. 1942.

ABOVE Tom Wong splits wood to add to the pile his mother has already chopped, c. 1956. PHOTOS COURTESY OF DR. TOM WONG

When I was older, I would go off to play with my friends in the woods, climbing young cedar trees that would bend over until we could touch the ground, jump off, and let them whip back up to the sky. We didn't have any fishing rods, but we would head to Comox Lake, go out on rafts, and fish with cedar poles. We used about sixteen feet of catgut as a fishing line and we hooked worms for bait. We would throw rocks at targets of cans and bottles, and later we used BB guns to hit our targets. One man paid us three cents for a robin and four cents for a blue jay; he would roast these small birds for his dinner. I developed a good throwing arm and was the pitcher on my high school softball team.

I have fond memories of those simple times with my friends: Norman Leung, who lived with his uncle, Ken Lowe, and grandmother in Cumberland's Chinatown until he was older and had to work in the family grocery store in town, and Charlie Mah, until his family moved to Vancouver in 1939. Jack Chow, who was the youngest in his family, would come with us if his mother let him go out to play. Jack moved to Vancouver with his family when we were in about grade ten. Years later, as young adults in Vancouver, I was evicted for standing up for a friend who was inappropriately evicted by our landlord, and Jack let me stay at his place.

Kids of all ages would gather for tea and snacks at Marie Mah's home, where she lived with her father, Kim Mah. He would study the rules and organize our basketball, softball, and soccer games. We all shared a catcher's mitt.

Ken Lowe's home had the only radio in Chinatown. We would gather at his place to listen to *Amos and Andy*, *The Shadow*, and on Sundays, Harvey Lowe's show on Chinese culture, *The Call of China*.

The Kindness of Mrs. Finch

One person who had a huge impact on the lives of all of us in Cumberland's Chinatown was Lydia Katherine Finch. She was our Sunday school teacher at the Anglican Mission Church that was down the street from my home. She played the organ for the Cumberland Anglican Church and gave piano lessons. She would do all she could to help newcomers to Chinatown feel welcomed. Her personal mission was to help the Chinese community.

An intelligent and artistic individual, Mrs. Finch generously shared her time and talent with us. She did this day after day, brightening our lives with her lovely, warm presence. After school,

ABOVE Lydia Katherine Finch (*centre, wearing hat*), Sunday school teacher at the Anglican Mission Church in Cumberland, poses with former students and their families during a reunion in 1951. COURTESY OF DR. TOM WONG

from four until six o'clock, she taught us English through a variety of activities including singing, art, and Bible study. She taught us what was right and wrong, nurturing our virtues and shaping our values.

When we were born, our parents gave us Chinese names. Mrs. Finch gave each of us the English first names that we would use for the rest of our lives. Most of them sounded similar to our Chinese names. By the time we started school in Cumberland, we were known by our English names. Our new names and the gift of speaking English helped us tremendously when we began our lives outside Chinatown.

Another generous individual who helped our community was Mr. George Apps, the principal at the Cumberland Elementary School. Every week, Mr. Apps would conduct the children's Sunday service at the Anglican Mission Church. He supported the Japanese community in Cumberland as well and kept in touch with the kids who had to move to internment camps during the Second World War.

ABOVE Tom Wong (*standing, fifth from left*) with his fellow Comox Valley Sea Cadets during a summer camp at Whytecliff Park in West Vancouver, c. 1944.
COURTESY OF DR. TOM WONG

Fitting In

Although there was a lot of racism when I was growing up in Cumberland, I tried not to let it get to me. There was some name-calling in the early years of school, but after standing up to bullies, I didn't have any other problems. Outside of school, we Chinese kids didn't socialize with our Caucasian classmates. We never visited their homes. It wasn't due to prejudice, and we weren't anti-social. We were just too busy. We had to spend time with Mrs. Finch, walk the one mile back to Chinatown, and do our chores.

One of the few Caucasian kids I hung out with was Alvin Tantrum, who was my partner for the three-legged race on Empire Day each year. Empire Day was a big celebration in town, with a parade and races with cash prizes for all age groups. When I was a teen, a day's winnings could be as high as forty dollars (big money for a poor kid in the 1940s). There was the slow bicycle race, the winner being the one who finished last without falling; the hundred-yard dash; the high jump, which involved landing

on gravel—I had a record jump of five feet seven inches; and the three-legged race.

I played soccer with the other kids at school, borrowing Billy Rallison's soccer cleats for tournaments. The Watson family would lend me running spikes on Sports Day, even though I was competing against Leland Watson.

During the Second World War, a dozen kids from the region and I would get picked up in a big canvas-covered military truck on Friday nights for Sea Cadet training in Comox. We had lots of fun and learned to tie knots, row large whaler boats, and shoot rifles. I enjoyed the summer camps at the HMS *Discovery* in Stanley Park and Whytecliff Park in West Vancouver.

After graduating from high school, I attended the Dominion-Provincial Youth Training Centre to study auto mechanics. The principal had come to our high school to recruit students. The vocational school was founded in downtown Nanaimo in 1936 and moved to the site of an old army camp in 1946, the year before I attended. It later became Malaspina College and

ABOVE Dominion-Provincial Youth Training Centre class of 1950. Tom Wong (*front row, third from the left*) studied auto mechanics at the Nanaimo Vocational School (the precursor to today's Vancouver Island University).
COURTESY OF DR. TOM WONG

eventually Vancouver Island University. Tuition was free, and I paid a dollar a day for meals on weekdays.

I was the top student in my class and won the prize of the five-hundred-dollar Snap-on toolkit. It was presented to me by the service manager of Vancouver Motors, who offered me a job. I moved to Vancouver and worked at Vancouver Motors, earning ninety cents per hour for the first year. In Vancouver, I hung around with Fred Soo, who was the top student at the Dominion Provincial Vocational School the year after me and was working at Johnson Motors. He told me that his friend from Nanaimo, John Wong, was in medical school.

Like my mother, I was good at working with my hands and solving problems, so I set my sights on dentistry, saved my money, and earned my bachelor of science degree at the University of British Columbia.

I met my future wife, Ina, through the Mei Wun Choristers, who met at the Chinese Benevolent Association Building in Vancouver's Chinatown. After choral practice, our group would hang out in a nearby café. Ina was born in the Strathcona neighbourhood of Vancouver and worked as a clerk stenographer at Gladstone Secondary School. We married in 1956.

Our first son, Colin, was born in 1958, the same year that I moved to Montreal to study dentistry at McGill University, and for the first year, I stayed at the YMCA. Ina and Colin joined me during my second year, and during my third and fourth years, Ina worked for the Protestant School Board in Montreal. My friend Dr. John Wong, who was specializing in otolaryngology, used to drive me to the university, and Colin had his tonsillectomy at the hospital where John worked. I graduated and started my dental practice in 1962, the year our second son, Davidicus, was born. Our daughter, Lisa, was born in 1964.

Our grandson Ryan, a fourth-generation Chinese Canadian, lives in Honolulu. Hawaii has always been a favourite vacation place for our family. It is one of the few places in the world where we are treated as locals and are only expected to speak English.

No one makes snap judgments about us based on race and asks, "Where are you from? . . . No, I mean, where are you *really* from?"

Growing up in the 1930s and '40s and settling into our families and careers in the 1950s and '60s, we just wanted to be seen and accepted as equals—as Canadians first and Chinese second.

The Challenge of Learning English

As second-generation Chinese Canadians, we were discouraged from speaking English at home. Our immigrant parents didn't want us speaking what they could not understand. Most of my friends and I had to repeat grade one because of our poor English at the time. Thanks to Mrs. Finch's afterschool lessons, we all learned to speak fluent English without an accent.

English was a barrier to higher education for many of my generation. My brother, though bright, was unable to get a degree at UBC because he could not pass the English competency test. That test remained a challenge for decades of students who spoke English as a second language.

When Ina and I were raising our children in the 1960s, we wanted them to fit in and succeed in contributing to the wider Canadian society. We decided to speak only English at home. Not just good enough English to get by with in everyday life but perfect English. We even kept my university dictionary by the kitchen table to settle debates about the correct pronunciation or usage of words. We also deliberately did not teach our children the peasant-version of the Cantonese dialect our parents taught us.

When our children were in elementary school, there were very few Chinese families in our Burnaby neighbourhood. We couldn't have imagined the dramatic influx of Asian immigration in the coming decades that would make it an advantage to be multilingual.

I practised dentistry in Burnaby for fifty-two years, retiring at age eighty-four. My sons graduated from UBC with medical degrees. Colin worked for many years as an anesthesiologist in

Vernon and remains active in his church community. Davidicus is a family physician and writer; he is committed to improving the health of the community. He helped me write this chapter.

My daughter, Lisa, graduated in kinesiology from Simon Fraser University and has a successful business as a financial planner and insurance broker. She has been contributing to the Richmond community for over two decades now. She has served on the board of the Richmond Chamber of Commerce, acted as chair of the Business Excellence Awards Committee, is a past board member of Richmond Cares, Richmond Gives, and has volunteered many times to raise money for the Christmas Fund.

I have seven grandchildren, all young adults finding their place in life and contributing to Canadian society with no barriers. My grandson Adam was born 100 years after my father came to Cumberland. As individuals, families, and a nation, we have come a long way.

The First Cumberland Chinatown Reunions

Around 1972, we surprised Mrs. Finch for her eightieth birthday. Many of her former students gathered in Courtenay to give her a big thank-you for the tremendous impact she had on our lives. After that, the Cumberland Chinatown reunions became a regular occurrence. We enjoyed meeting up with old friends, sharing memories, and celebrating how far we and our families had come.

Because Cumberland's Chinatown no longer exists and most of us had moved to the Lower Mainland, we held our annual picnics in Stanley Park near the miniature railway in the early years. In more recent years, we've gathered at the picnic site at Riverfront Park overlooking the Fraser River in South Vancouver.

Today, it may seem hard to imagine that at one time, we who were born in Canada were not considered citizens, did not have the right to vote, were excluded from many professions, were paid less than other races, and were forbidden by race-based exclusionary acts to reunite our families in this country.

During the Second World War, my oldest sister, Lila, who was eighteen at the time, enlisted in the military, as did many Chinese Canadians who wanted to serve our country and hoped to have Canadian-born Chinese recognized as voting citizens.

In February 1947, at a ceremony in Vancouver's Commodore Ballroom, Lila was among the first seven Chinese Canadians to be granted Canadian citizenship.

We all owe a debt of gratitude to the early Chinese Canadian pioneers, the cohesive caring community of Cumberland's Chinatown, our friends, and the committed kindness of special people like Mrs. Finch.

8

The Trees Will Remember Irene

DAWN COPEMAN

It starts as a small white knob, or sometimes several, on the trunk of a standing dead tree. Visually, it is somewhat reminiscent of a marshmallow or small cream puff, but it is hard to the touch. As the growth swells in size, small beads of moisture, called guttation, appear on the surface, signalling a rapid growth phase. The top flattens out a bit and an orange blush colour appears in the white bulbous growth. Sometimes it assumes a plate shape, and other times it stays knobby, resembling a nose or a hoof. Over time—days, weeks, years—the surface darkens to an ashy grey or dark brown. The upper surface has ring upon ring of ridges and can be shiny or dull. New growth typically shows as a red belt with a yellow band around the outer ring, fringed with a white rind.

The commonly named red-belted conk, originally identified as *Fomes pinicola* in scholarly studies of the fungus from the late 1920s by Dr. Irene Mounce and more recently as *Fomitopsis pinicola*,

ABOVE *Fomitopsis mounceae*, a species of red-belted conk, grows in the Cumberland Forest. The fungi was identified in 2019 and named after Dr. Irene Mounce, the pioneering plant pathologist born in Union, BC, in 1894. COURTESY OF DAWN COPEMAN

is a perennial fungus and one of the most common bracket fungi in the forests around Cumberland. In 2019, DNA analysis determined there were actually four different species of *Fomitopsis*, two of which occur in British Columbia. *Fomitopsis mounceae*, one of the two newly identified species, was named in honour of Dr. Mounce, a Canadian pioneer plant pathologist born in Cumberland.

As the red-belted conk is showing itself on the outside of a tree, it is spreading itself inward as well. It absorbs nutrients from within the tree as the mycelium network mines deep into the cellulose and heartwood and transforms the tree from a potential source of lumber into chunks of soft, punky wood. Brown rot breaks down its internal structure. Bugs move in, and birds, bears, and other creatures excavate the soft innards in search of food or shelter. In forest time, the whole woody ecosystem gradually disintegrates into the forest floor.

Spores from the red-belted conk spread themselves over long distances, successfully implanting in sick and wounded trees, filling spaces with "wefts of white mycelium," as Mounce described it in a 1929 paper. Snags, deadfalls, and scars caused by windstorms or forest fires are all potential hosts. Moving from tree to tree, conks are a very efficient forest decomposition tool. They accelerate decay as part of a cooperative forest network that keeps the forest functioning. Rotted trees create holes in the mature forest canopy for light, promoting new growth. Rot and regeneration keep the forest ecosystem in balance.

If you see a forest only in economic terms, you don't want to see fungi growing on trees. They signify decay and are the enemy of profit. Tree pathology and the study of tree diseases grew out of a desire to understand and conquer this enemy. Dr. Mounce researched tree pathogens for most of her twenty-five-year career with the federal Department of Agriculture.

IRENE MOUNCE WAS BORN into privilege in Union, BC, in 1894. Her father, Lewis Mounce, was a prosperous lumberman and accountant with investments up and down Vancouver Island. In the late 1880s, his interests already included livery stables, blacksmiths, the Shawnigan Lake Lumber Company, and several sawmill operations. He was a partner in two mills and other endeavours in Wellington and Union (later Cumberland) with Robert Grant. When the Wellington mill was sold, Lewis built a fine, large house on Derwent Avenue in Union and moved his young family north. His wife, Euphemia, and their baby, Leland Grant, were later joined by Irene, Marion, and Lewis, all born at home in Union.

Robert Grant took care of the technical side of the mill operations and Lewis Mounce ran the business side. The sawmill processed twenty thousand board feet of lumber a day, supplied the mines with railway ties and pit props, and milled all the wood to build houses for the growing community. Trees were everywhere. Many heritage houses standing in the village today have knot-free fir flooring in twenty-four-foot lengths, made at the Grant & Company mill.

Lewis Mounce was contracted to clear land, build streets, and manage farms and rental properties. He became the first mayor of the city of Cumberland in January 1898 and was later an MLA for the District. An 1897 photo shows Lewis Mounce and his wife and children, along with other early Cumberland VIPs, at the site of the new Cumberland & Union Waterworks. In the photo, big trees are still visible, but there are also a lot of large stumps with springboard scars. Cumberland was surrounded by forest—and Grant & Company intended to log it all.

ABOVE Cumberland VIPs and their family members gathered at the site of the new Cumberland & Union Waterworks in July 1897. Lewis Mounce, lumberman and future first mayor of Cumberland, is standing third from the right in the back row beside two ladies in hats. Euphemia, Irene, and Leland Mounce are also present. COURTESY OF DARYL CALNAN

Logging then was not as systematic as it is now, less "clear cut." There was a lot of hewing, hand-sawing, and brute labour, with logs hauled by teams of horses. All that work to develop a raw, ugly mining camp with muddy, unpaved streets, surrounded by a wasteland of stumps and slash and coal dust. A few large trees were left standing: trees with split trunks, trees too big in diameter for the blades at the sawmill, a lot of cedar, which was not considered valuable, and trees with signs of disease—a few lonely sentinels to remember the forest that once was.

Lumbermen are always on the lookout for diseased trees. While Lewis Mounce looked for rotten logs in the woodlots, his children played in the stumps and remaining forest just steps from their home. And it was here, in the slash and forests of Cumberland, that Irene developed her lifelong interest in tree diseases, fungus, and bacteriology.

On August 12, 1912, the R. Grant & Company Sawmill in Cumberland burned to the ground. Lewis Mounce had moved to Vancouver in 1911, and so he avoided the fire—as well as the two-year labour dispute involving all the Vancouver Island coal mines and the financing problems that came with rebuilding the mill when it was relocated to Royston. The partnership between Grant and Mounce dissolved in December 1917, but the families remained friends, and Lewis Mounce and his family continued to summer at their cottage on Gartley Beach in Royston in the Comox Valley.

It was an interesting time in British Columbia. The Big Strike was raging up and down Vancouver Island, and thousands of coal miners were locked out of the mines and evicted from company housing. Some were living on the beach, just a short distance from the Mounce summer residence. Vancouver was a different world, far removed from the labour movement roiling in Cumberland.

Moving to Vancouver provided many more educational and cultural opportunities for the Mounce children. However, you can take the girl out of Cumberland, but you can't take Cumberland out of the girl. It must have been a culture shock to the Mounce girls to go from bushwhacking around the forest to playing piano, having genteel teas, and attending normal school. Leland was groomed to take over the lumber business, but there was no similar expectation—or opportunity—for female children at the time. Irene was a very intelligent young woman who wanted more than the status quo.

In the years before the Great War, the expectations for a young woman of Irene's class were clear: good works at the church, or at a charity for some "worthy" cause, and possibly further education, teach for a few years, and then find a suitable husband. Irene graduated from normal school in Vancouver in 1912. Whether she taught for a short time or not is not documented, but she became interested in the Pioneer Political Equality League, and in 1914, she served tea to fundraise for the women's suffrage movement.

The war upended everything. While conflict raged in Europe, there was a small window of opportunity for Irene to convince her parents that times were changing and that there were no young men around for her to marry anyway, so funding more education was a good way to keep her occupied and happy. In 1915, she registered as a student at the newly opened University of British Columbia (UBC), where she blossomed. According to the 1918 issue of the UBC student annual, "Irene's outstanding characteristics are an ability to obtain first class marks with no effort and an almost unlimited capacity for cream puffs. . . . She is equally devoted to Bacteriology, Botany and Hoy's Bakery."

Science was not something that ladies studied, but an exception was made for botany, which wasn't considered a serious science at the time. Pressing flowers and collecting ferns were acceptable pastimes, however, and if you wanted to label your collection with the proper Latin names, even better.

As a lumberman's daughter, Irene gravitated toward studying subjects bigger than ferns and wildflowers, and she spent much of her academic and working career investigating tree disease. She graduated with a BA, majoring in Bacteriology and Latin. She was the top student in the first-ever graduating class at UBC in 1918 and won the Governor General's Gold Medal. She continued her education with an MA (1920) from UBC, followed by an MSc (1922) from the University of Manitoba and a PhD (1929) from the University of Toronto. Dr. Mounce was the first woman in Canada to graduate from studies in agriculture with anything higher than a bachelor's degree. She was awarded fellowships and opportunities to study under the pre-eminent mushroom and tree disease specialists of the day, supporting herself along the way through scholarships and lab work.

In 1922, the *Winnipeg Tribune* published an article titled "Manitoba Girl Savant Speaks." Irene, then a research fellow at the University of Manitoba, read a paper at the convention of the Association for the Advancement of Science about the mating properties of mycelia produced by spores in some species of *Coprinus* (shaggy mane). Describing Irene as a savant seems wrong to modern ears, but at the time it was an accolade. A savant, according to one Oxford dictionary, was "a very learned or talented person, especially one distinguished in a particular field of science or the arts." A recognized smarty-pants, in other words.

ABOVE Irene Mounce (*back left*) poses with six fellow students the University of British Columbia at its original Fairview location in 1915. Mounce was among the first students to graduate from the new university. COURTESY OF UBC ARCHIVES PHOTOGRAPH COLLECTION

Irene was appointed assistant plant pathologist in the forestry branch of the civil service in Ottawa in April 1924. In the summer of 1924 she travelled to the Queen Charlotte Islands (now Haida Gwaii) to collect samples of fungus from Western hemlocks and Sitka spruce. This field study was a continuation of her earlier research at the Timber Testing Laboratory in Vancouver for the Imperial Munitions Board. Her Master's thesis from UBC was titled "Some Factors Affecting the Commercial Value of Spruce Wood."

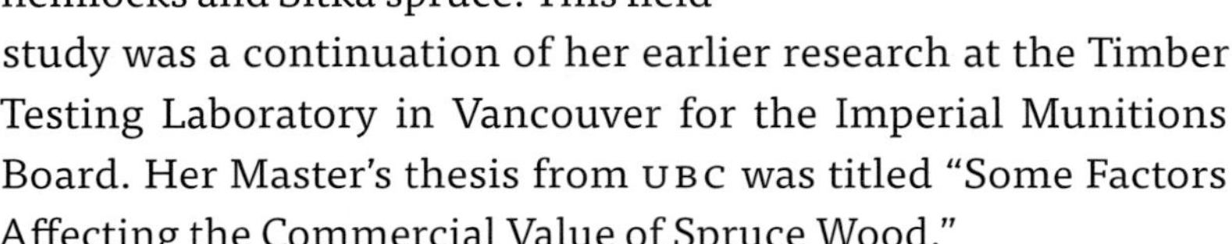

Old-growth Sitka spruce was being logged and shipped to the UK to build planes, but much of the expensive lumber was unusable by the time it arrived due to the effects of some unidentified disease. Identifying and preventing disease required getting samples of the sporophores (the spore-bearing structure of the fungus—the conk) from the trunks of Western hemlocks and Sitka spruce where they grew. The samples were then brought back to the labs at the Central Experimental Research Farm in Ottawa for propagation on various cultures and detailed analysis. These samples and the interpretation of the results of the tests on them formed the basis of Irene's graduate thesis at the University of Toronto.

It is challenging enough to get to Haida Gwaii today, but it was a veritable expedition in the 1920s. Imagine, after several days of travelling by train and boat, tromping through the bush with a small haversack containing a hatchet, paper bags to hold your specimens, field notes, and lunch. You are wearing stout, sensible shoes, and possibly carrying a walking pole to assist you over the rough ground as you search for disease samples in the forest, taking care to keep mud off your long skirt. This is definitely the path less travelled for a youngish single woman, and far from the botany hobby imagined by your father.

Botany was the first branch of science to provide a career for Canadian women. Still, unmarried women, highly skilled or not, were generally not welcomed with open arms by the greater scientific community and were often relegated to less prestigious positions and paid less than their male counterparts.

Dr. Mounce's dissertation was published by the Dominion of Canada Department of Agriculture in 1929. In the Dominion Experimental Farms employee directory there are only two women: Irene, on staff as an assistant plant pathologist in Ottawa, and Margaret Newton, Senior Plant Pathologist under J.H. Craigie, who is identified as Senior Plant Pathologist *in charge* at the Winnipeg Dominion Rust Research Laboratory and, like everyone else in the directory, identified only by his initials plus surname. Only the two women on staff are more familiarly identified by their first names. Both have doctorates. The Senior Plant Pathologist "in charge" in Manitoba didn't get his PhD until eight years after Dr. Newton received hers.

Dr. H.T. Güssow, the Dominion Botanist, was vocal in his disapproval of women working in his lab, but even he had to accept that Irene Mounce was a talented, excellent researcher. Irene even persuaded him to hire a second woman to work in the Ottawa lab, Mildred K. Nobles, as a summer student in 1929. Irene encouraged Mildred to go on to graduate work. After she completed her studies, Mildred had a long and illustrious career at the Department of Agriculture in the Botany Lab, eventually surpassing her mentor in prominence within the mycology community.

Irene continued her work with brown rot throughout the 1930s. She also undertook studies to determine why eelgrass in New Brunswick was declining and isolated the fungus causing the problem. She learned new lab techniques and continued undertaking field studies to supply material for the newly created Ottawa Herbarium (now the Canadian National Mycological

Herbarium, more commonly known as the DAOM, short for Department of Agriculture, Ottawa, Mycology). She oversaw the development of the National Wood Decay Fungi Herbarium, where her samples are still used today.

At the beginning of the Second World War, Irene was loaned to the Dominion Laboratory of Plant Pathology at Saanichton, BC, to work on seed-borne diseases that were affecting vegetable crops. While she was there, she recommended that a forest pathology lab be established at the Central Experimental Farm at Lake Cowichan and also established a regional herbarium.

THE RECOGNITION AND RESPECT from her peers and the increasing responsibility she assumed over several years as a career civil servant all paint a vivid picture of Irene as an academic and a scientist, but what about Irene personally? Irene the woman is a mystery.

We have just the bare bones of what she was like as a person outside the laboratory. We know she played varsity tennis at UBC, loved cream puffs as an undergraduate, poured tea for the Imperial Daughters of the Empire (now the IODE) in Winnipeg, and put in a word to have Mildred hired at the botany lab in Ottawa. Irene came west most years to visit her family when she worked in Ottawa. She was close to her sister Marion, who was awarded an MA in Agriculture from UBC and taught there until her marriage to Howard Green in 1923.

Irene chose a career instead of marriage. At that time, many jobs available to white middle-class women were subject to a marriage bar. For female scientists in the civil service, and many other white-collar occupations, if you married, you were "required to resign," Cindy Stelmackowich wrote in a 2019 paper. A memo from the Privy Council Office of the Public Service Commission dated June 18, 1920, makes this crystal clear: "Hereafter no married woman, whose husband is living, shall be eligible for appointment in the Public Service."

When she was working with seeds in Saanich, Dr. Mounce got to know Gordon MacLeod Stewart, a fifty-seven-year-old widower with grown children who lived in Vancouver. He was the Dominion seed inspector for Alberta and BC. In 1945, at age fifty, she married him and was "required to resign." She moved from Saanich to Vancouver after she married.

Despite her successes as a scientist, Irene does not seem to have maintained contact with her former colleagues after she resigned from the civil service. Her life from 1945 until her death in 1987 is not documented. Mycologists in Ottawa and Vancouver are aware of her published work, but no one remembers ever meeting her at any group or seminar in Vancouver. It's possible she kept in touch with Mildred Nobles, but contact could have been limited to exchanging Christmas cards. I hope Irene shared her love of the forest with her grandchildren by marriage and embraced family life to the fullest, with no regrets.

When she died in 1987, her obituary in the publication *Mycologia* described her as diligent and insightful, breaking new ground in mycology and paving the way for female scientists like Mildred Nobles (who never married) to continue her work. Her obituary in the *Vancouver Sun* was not only very brief but also mentioned nothing about her career.

FOREST MANAGEMENT IS a big industry in BC, and the work of trying to identify and understand how tree diseases spread and how to prevent infection continues today. As long as there are forests—and logging—studying plant pathology will remain a priority.

There are still some old cedar stumps visible in the forests around Cumberland today, neighbours of trees logged 130 years ago by Irene's father, that haven't succumbed to complete decay. The stumps and slash have transformed over time into a beautiful mature mixed second-growth forest. That forest won't be logged. The land surrounding the Village of Cumberland has been purchased by the villagers as a community forest.

There will always be red-belted conks doing the job of breaking down rotten wood. Thousands of generations of spore fall of *Fomitopsis mounceae*, appearing as small cream puffs on the bark of dead trees, continue doing their part to sustain the life cycle of the forest. Lewis Mounce has a road named after him. The trees will remember Irene.

SOURCES

BARR, J. N. *Cumberland Heritage, A Selected History of People Buildings Institutions & Sites 1888-1950*, Corp. of the Village of Cumberland, 1997.

GINNS, J. "Irene Mounce, 1894–1987." *Mycologia* 80, no. 5 (September–October, 1988): 607-608. https://www.jstor.org/stable/3807707

HUGHES, S. J. "Obituary: Dr. Mildred K. Nobles." *The Forestry Chronicle* 74, no. 3 (May/June 1998). https://pubs.cif-ifc.org/doi/pdf/10.5558/tfc74446-3

MACKINNON, A. AND K. LUTHER. *Mushrooms of British Columbia*. Vancouver, BC: Royal BC Museum, 2021.

MOUNCE, IRENE. "Some Factors Affecting the Commercial Value of Spruce Wood." MA thesis, UBC, Faculty of Forestry, 1920. UBC Theses and Dissertations. https://open.library.ubc.ca/collections/ubctheses/831/items/1.0088720

MOUNCE, IRENE. *Studies of Forest Pathology: II. The Biology of Fomes Pinicola, (Sw.) Cooke*. Dominion of Canada, Department of Agriculture Bulletin no. 111. Ottawa: Department of Agriculture, 1929. https://oaresource.library.carleton.ca/wcl/201%20160519/A12-2-111-1929-eng.pdf

PROVINCIAL NORMAL SCHOOL (BC). "Provincial Normal School Year Book 1912-13." 1913. BC Historical Documents. http://dx.doi.org/10.14288/1.0370835.

STELMACKOWICH, CINDY. "Cultivating Knowledge about Canadian Women Scientists through Seminars, Objects, and Exhibitions." *Scientia Canadensis* 41, no. 1 (2019): 55-65. https://doi.org/10.7202/1065959ar

UBC 1918: The Third Annual of the University of British Columbia. Vancouver, BC: Publications Board of the Alma Mater Society [n.d.]. https://www.library.ubc.ca/archives/pdfs/yearbooks/1918_totem.pdf

VANCOUVER DAILY PROVINCE. The Daily Province's Page of Social and Personal News. May 20, 1914. https://theprovince.newspapers.com/paper/the-province/11702/

VANCOUVER DAILY PROVINCE. "Ottawa Post for Graduate of U.B.C." April 4, 1924. https://theprovince.newspapers.com/paper/the-province/11702/

VANCOUVER SUN. "Irene (née Mounce) Stewart" [obituary]. July 10, 1987. https://www.newspapers.com/paper/the-vancouver-sun/11420/

WINNIPEG EVENING TRIBUNE. "Manitoba Girl Savant Speaks." January 3, 1922. https://digitalcollections.lib.umanitoba.ca/islandora/object/uofm%3A1549633

9

Cumberland Chow Mein

A Legacy of Dreams and Determination

RUSSELL SAKAUYE

Throughout the years, family events and gatherings have served as cherished milestones, bringing together generations of the Ogaki family. Food often played a starring role at these events, and one dish in particular held a special place in our hearts: Cumberland chow mein. From countless family birthday parties to Father's Day Buddhist Church picnics at Caledon Place, this dish became a symbol of togetherness and an enduring legacy of the former Japanese Canadian residents of the town of Cumberland, British Columbia.

As a child, I savoured each bite of Cumberland chow mein, never realizing its deep-rooted connection to my grandfather's past. It wasn't until 2011, when I was writing an article in the Japanese Canadian newspaper the NAJC *Bulletin*, that I began to explore the history and origins of my beloved dish. Research then was difficult due to the lack of online resources, but I learned a lot from my grandmother, Mae (née Nagano) Ogaki, who was more willing to talk about the past than my grandfather and who grew up in Duncan prior to the internment. The passing of my grandfather, Tame "Buzz" Ogaki, in November 2022 at the age of ninety-nine then led to an invitation to contribute a story to this book. Thus began another trip through records and stories of my grandfather's family. I had better access to online resources than I had in 2011, plus a hunger to uncover more details about the Ogaki family's journey from Japan to Canada; their life in Cumberland; and their internment, migration, and settlement in Toronto.

My grandfather's friend Stoney Sora nicknamed him Buzz after a popular hockey player. Buzz was a man of few words when it came to his past. He preferred to focus on the present, immersing himself in playing sports, coaching teams, and providing for his wife, Mae, and six children. Through my grandmother's accounts, interviews my mom conducted with my grandmother, and the University of Victoria's Landscapes of Injustice project, I pieced together fragments of the Ogakis' experience in Cumberland and the hardships they endured.

My personal memories associated with Cumberland chow mein became a gateway to a deeper understanding of my family's history. I enjoyed it at family gatherings on the same types of occasions when my father's grandmother, my great-grandmother Maki, would have served it to her boys.

IN THE EARLY 1900S, Asaji Kadoki left his homeland of Japan aboard the *Nippon Maru* to seek new opportunities in Canada. At five feet two and eighteen years old, he was filled with hopes and dreams when he left behind his only family in Okayama, looking to build a family of his own and make a name for himself as Asaji Ogaki. Asaji had been adopted by his eldest sister's in-laws, the Ogaki family in Okayama, an area between Hiroshima and Osaka. He carried the Ogaki name with pride, honour, and aspirations for a brighter future.

Arriving in Canada in 1907, he found logging work on Vancouver Island near Victoria, BC. Five years later, in 1912, his future bride and beloved, Maki Tokimitsu, immigrated to Canada. Both Buddhist, they married at the Methodist Church in Victoria on July 4, 1913, and began their life together. They moved to the Steveston area, and soon after welcomed their first two sons, Hajime and then Takashi "Tak," into the world.

Before Tak was born, Asaji and Maki travelled back to Japan, where they left six-month-old Hajime in the care of Asaji's eldest sister on the Ogaki farm in Okayama. During the Second World War, because he was the male heir to the Ogaki family and a farmer, and therefore crucial to the domestic war effort, Hajime was not conscripted. My mother recalled a story my grandma shared with her: Hajime was working in a field one day, when suddenly he felt something warm on the back of his neck. He had been burned by radiation from the hydrogen bomb dropped on nearby Hiroshima, August 6, 1945. He would bear the scars on his neck for the rest of his life. After the war and the passing of his aunt, Hajime sold the farm and in 1952 moved back to his birth country of Canada with his wife and two children.

Sometime between 1916 and 1918, filled with anticipation and uncertainty, the Ogakis travelled to Cumberland as part of a wave of Japanese immigrants who sought opportunities in the forestry and coal-mining industries on Vancouver Island. Already proficient in English thanks to the Methodist and Buddhist Churches, they quickly settled into their new community, the No. 5 Japanese Town just southwest of Maple Lake. Cultures intertwined throughout the Cumberland community, and people from diverse backgrounds worked side by side, creating a vibrant and lively atmosphere.

Cumberland's roots were in the coal industry. However, logging played a significant role in the settlement of Vancouver Island as a whole, and several logging companies had already established themselves in town when the Ogakis arrived. Asaji was able to leverage his skills and experience, working diligently in the local logging industry.

ABOVE The Ogaki Boys (except Hajime, who was living in Japan at the time) pose for a photo in Cumberland on May 24, 1938. *Front row, left to right:* Jogi, Buzz, Toshiaki, Katsumi, Sueyoshi. *Back row:* Tak, Tsuyoshi, Hiroshi. COURTESY OF RUSSELL SAKAUYE

Meanwhile, Maki embraced her role as a loving mother and homemaker, tending to their growing brood with warmth and care. Their family expanded as they welcomed another seven sons: Hiroshi "Rosie," Jogi "George," Sueyoshi "Chops," Tame "Buzz," Tsuyoshi "Chips," Katsumi "Charlie," and Toshiaki "Tosh," all born in Cumberland. Each boy brought joy and laughter to the Ogaki household.

At some point, a man from Cumberland's Chinatown taught the Cumberland Japanese Women's Association, or Fujinkai, how to cook chow mein noodles and other dishes using the available ingredients. These lessons were rumoured to have been at one of the restaurants in No. 1 Japanese Town (named due to its location next to the No. 1 Coal Mine) or at one of the churches. That chow mein would connect generations of Japanese Canadians across Canada at many a picnic, family gathering, and celebration to come.

The boys thrived in Cumberland, enjoying the simple pleasures of childhood in a close-knit community and forming connections with other children. Summers were filled with picnics and events near picturesque Comox Lake, where families from all parts of the community gathered to share laughter and create lasting memories. After the war, Rosie married his childhood sweetheart, Hiroko "Judy" Matsubuchi, who was also born in Cumberland.

Faith and community played a significant role in the Ogaki family's life in Cumberland. Despite their Japanese Buddhist faith, the family found solace and support in the United Church at No. 5 Japanese Town. The United Church became a place where they could come together with other families and share in the values of compassion, unity, and fellowship. Next to the church was the baseball field, where the Ogaki boys spent much of their free time playing a sport that became an integral part of their family values.

THE DEEP BAY LOGGING COMPANY offered opportunity and growth for Japanese Canadians in Cumberland. The founder of the company was a Japanese immigrant named Eikichi Kagetsu, who, like Asaji, came to Canada looking for new opportunities and became a miner and logger. In the early 1920s, Kagetsu purchased 885 acres of forest land in Deep Bay, incorporating his new business venture as the Deep Bay Logging Co. on August 5, 1922. A year later, Kagheetsu purchased an additional three thousand acres of forest at Fanny Bay.

It's not known when Asaji began working for Kagetsu, but a 1921 census stated that he was earning one thousand dollars a month working in the logging industry as a teamster, and records show he was employed by Deep Bay Logging at the time of his internment in 1942.

The company that provided for Asaji's family also greatly contributed to the town's economic development. Logging became the lifeblood of the burgeoning Japanese Canadian community. As the Ogaki boys each came of age, they eagerly followed in their

HILLCR

ABOVE Japanese Canadian lumber workers in Hillcrest, BC, June 1940—less than two years before their internment during the Second World War. The author's great-grandfather Asaji is on the far left of the second row, and his grandfather Buzz and great-uncle Tak are in the third row, second and fourth from the left, respectively. COURTESY OF KAZUMASA AND MIYOKO HAMASAKI

father's footsteps and joined the ranks of the Deep Bay Logging Company. At the age of sixteen, Buzz, the youngest of the Ogaki boys to work for the company at the time, embraced the life of a lumberjack and log driver. With axe in hand and determination in his eyes, he fearlessly faced the challenges of the dangerous industry, honing his skills and building a strong physique in the process. He always claimed log-driving helped train his legs to run fast for baseball and hockey.

When not engaged in the demanding tasks of logging, the Ogaki boys revelled in the activities of Cumberland's community. Summers at Comox Lake were a time when families from all walks of life gathered for picnics and celebrations. They played baseball games in the diamond adjacent to the Japanese United Church, the air filled with cheers and laughter. In winter, they laced up their skates and played hockey on nearby Maple Lake. They listened to Toronto Maple Leafs games on the radio and eventually were inspired to choose Toronto as a place to settle after leaving Cumberland and the internment camps.

A major fire broke out in July 1927 at No. 5 Japanese Town. Twenty-six houses were destroyed, including the Ogakis' rental home. As a result, they were temporarily housed in the United Church until they could find new accommodation. Japanese Canadian families, many of whom worked at the Royston Lumber Mill, organized a benefit concert in Royston to help those affected by the fire.

Several more major fires happened in Cumberland in the following years. The terrifying experience of both the initial fire and the subsequent ones left Maki with trauma that stayed with her for the rest of her life.

Despite these setbacks, the Ogaki boys continued to work in the logging industry, primarily with the Deep Bay Logging Company and also for a time with Hillcrest Lumber Company, and carried with them the values instilled by their father. Their work in the forest, with its challenges and rewards, became the backdrop of their young adult lives, shaping their characters and laying the foundation for their future endeavours.

ABOVE The Hillcrest Lumber Co. baseball team, the Hillcrest Rangers, including Buzz (*front row, third from left*) and Tak (*front row, far right*), June 1940. COURTESY OF KAZUMASA AND MIYOKO HAMASAKI

FOLLOWING THE ATTACK on Pearl Harbor in December 1942, the Ogaki family were among the twenty-two thousand Japanese Canadians labelled "Enemy Aliens." Their lives were upturned by the forced relocation and internment enacted by the provincial and federal governments, and they were scattered across Canada, forever uprooted from the familiarity of their homes on Vancouver Island.

Asaji, Maki, and their three youngest children—Tsuyoshi, Katsumi, and Toshiaki—were living in Cumberland when this happened. Asaji was sent to a labour camp in Hope, on the eastern end of the Lower Mainland region of BC. Maki and the boys were transported to the Pacific National Exhibition (PNE) grounds at Hastings Park in East Vancouver. They and over eight thousand other Japanese Canadians endured fear and uncertainty, unsanitary accommodation, and cruel guards prior to being shipped off to various internment and labour camps in the province.

Maki and the boys ended up in the purpose-built camp of Tashme, the largest of the eight internment camps, near Hope.

Tak had been living in Hillcrest, BC, west of Duncan, before he was forcibly uprooted from his community and relocated to a labour camp in Schreiber, Ontario.

Both Hiroshi "Rosie" and Jogi "George" had built a life for themselves in the coastal town of Woodfibre, BC, south of Squamish, where they worked for the B.C. Pulp & Paper Company. Rosie was transported to a labour camp in London, Ontario, and George, like Tak, was sent to Schreiber.

Sueyoshi "Chops" was living with his family in Duncan, BC, and working for the Deep Bay Logging Company. My grandfather, Buzz, was living in Hillcrest with Tak. Both Chops and Buzz were sent to Toronto, where they probably stayed at the YMCA. Records show that both Chops and Buzz were playing baseball in Toronto prior to the release of Japanese Canadians from internment in 1946, so it's possible they were given more freedom than many of their peers during this time.

During Maki's time in Tashme, far from the familiar town the family once called home, the legacy of Cumberland chow mein truly began to flourish. The recipe was passed on by the former Cumberland residents to the families in Tashme and other internment sites. As a result, it became a cherished part of culinary culture within the Japanese Canadian community. Today, many variations passed down through the generations are based on the original recipe shared by former locals of Cumberland's Japanese Towns.

THE CHALLENGES THE FAMILY faced during internment, the displacement from their homes, and the loss of their livelihoods could have broken their spirits. Instead, they overcame adversity to rebuild their lives in Toronto and establish a new sense of home.

When the Ogaki family arrived in Toronto, a city where Japanese families were scarce prior to 1941, their aspirations for a new beginning were met with challenges and discriminatory practices.

Toronto mayor F.J. Conboy, for example, had imposed a ban on Japanese Canadians living in the city between 1942 and 1945. Despite the many and varied obstacles, determined individuals sought sponsorship from businesses, churches, and compassionate individuals who believed in the Japanese Canadians' right to call Toronto home. Through their unwavering spirit, the Japanese Canadian population in Toronto grew to approximately five thousand by 1947—but it was 1948 before they were granted the right to own land or property in Ontario. As a result, many Japanese families sought refuge in Montreal, which was a predominantly anglophone city at the time.

The Ogaki family forged connections in Toronto with like-minded individuals who believed in fostering inclusivity and breaking down barriers. Churches, social groups, and multicultural organizations provided support and facilitated gatherings, such as dances, sports leagues, and group outings. The Japanese Canadian community became a tight-knit network of individuals, united by their shared experiences and determination to rebuild their lives. They held cultural events and initiatives that celebrated their heritage and fostered their identity. The multicultural nature of Toronto allowed for interactions and collaborations with other communities, enriching the fabric of the city and creating lasting connections.

The purchase of a house at 352 Huron Street was a significant milestone for the Ogaki family's settlement in Toronto. It symbolized stability and security and provided them with a place to call their own. The house, likely purchased in 1949, was paid off by 1953. It became a sanctuary where family memories were created and cherished. Owning their own home gave the Ogakis a renewed sense of hope and a foundation for their future as they rebuilt their lives.

Among the Ogaki brothers, Buzz faced unique challenges. Health issues, such as a bout of tuberculosis, posed obstacles, but his indomitable spirit prevailed. Supported by his family and friends, Buzz embarked on a path of personal growth and perseverance.

ABOVE Asaji and Maki Ogaki outside their home in Toronto on 352 Huron St. in the 1950s. COURTESY OF RUSSELL SAKAUYE

He embraced education, expanding his knowledge and skills. Throughout his employment experiences, from bookkeeping to project management, Buzz showed dedication and tenacity and left an indelible mark on those he worked with.

Amid his pursuits, Buzz found love and companionship in the form of Miyeko "Mae" Nagano. They married and started a family together, cherishing and promoting the values of love, respect, and unity. Buzz's involvement in coaching sports, including baseball and hockey, nurtured a love for sports in others and instilled a sense of camaraderie and teamwork.

Each Ogaki brother made notable contributions to the Japanese Canadian community in Toronto. Hajime, when he returned to Canada in 1952, played a significant role in the establishment of a Japanese store in Toronto's first Chinatown. Tak cultivated plant saplings, sold koi, and shared his expertise as an experienced lumberjack. George became a certified accountant, while Rosie and his wife, Judy Matsubuchi, opened a general store called Paramount in Greektown, Toronto. Buzz left his mark through his work as an office manager and his involvement in construction projects. Chips and Chops excelled as carpenters, even constructing large movie theatres. Tosh showcased his talent as an award-winning lampshade designer. Charlie's dedication to community-building led him to contribute to the creation of the Japanese Canadian Cultural Centre, during which he collaborated with the renowned architect Raymond Moriyama.

The Ogaki family's post-war settlement in Toronto is a testament to the enduring impact they have had on the Japanese Canadian community. Their legacy serves as a reminder of the importance of preserving heritage, fostering inclusivity, and celebrating the strength that lies within diversity. My grandfather embodied the values of hard work and dedication. He imparted these qualities through his coaching, teaching us the importance of teamwork, perseverance, and giving our best in every endeavour. His love of sports and his commitment to his family and community were an inspiration for all of us.

SOURCES

COPEMAN, DAWN. "Fire Fire Fire." Cumberland Museum and Archives. 2020. https://cumberlandmuseum.ca/fire-fire-fire/

KAGETSU, TADASHI J. *The Tree Trunk Can Be My Pillow: The Biography of an Outstanding Japanese Canadian*. Victoria, BC: University of Victoria, 2017. https://doi.org/10.1353/book.65887

SUNAHARA, ANN G. *The Politics of Racism*. Nikkei National Museum & Cultural Centre, 2020. http://japanesecanadianhistory.ca/chapter-4-exile/

Classic Cumberland Chow Mein Toronto-Style

SERVES 2–8 (DEPENDING ON AMOUNT OF NOODLES)

The nostalgic flavours of Cumberland chow mein bridge generations and have preserved the Ogaki family's cultural heritage. In the confines of the internment camps, where families from many different backgrounds were brought together, Cumberland chow mein provided comfort and a sense of shared identity. Through the injustice of internment, a humble dish hailing from the family's hometown on Vancouver Island emerged as a symbol of connection and new traditions. Its popularity soared, transcending the confines of the camp and becoming a beloved dish in Japanese Canadian culture across the country. As I pass down the recipe to future generations, I know that the legacy of the Ogaki family will continue to shape and inspire us all. Traditionally it's cooked in a *kinshi tamago* skillet (small rectangular pan), but you can use a small round pan.

Serve warm or cold for parties or picnics. A kids' favourite.

CHOW MEIN: INGREDIENTS

250 g (¼ lb) or up to 1 (1.4 kg) box dried Ya Ca Mein noodles (similar size to linguine)

Vegetable oil

Salt and black pepper

2 pork butt chops (or 500 g/½ lb char siu—Chinese BBQ pork), sliced into bite-sized pieces

1 white onion, chopped

3 celery sticks, thinly sliced

2 cloves garlic, minced

6–8 dried shiitake mushrooms (soaked overnight, drained, and sliced)

1 Tbsp julienned *beni shoga* (pickled red ginger)

Shoyu (for serving)

KINSHI TAMAGO (EGG TOPPING STRIPS)

3 eggs

1 Tbsp sugar

¼ Tbsp table salt

2 Tbsp vegetable oil

1 tsp cornstarch dissolved in 1 tsp water (optional)

CHOW MEIN: METHOD

1. To make the chow mein, fill a large Dutch oven three-quarters full with water and bring to a boil over high heat. Break the noodles in half and stir them into the water. Return the water to a boil over high heat, cook the noodles just until al dente, then drain. Do not rinse. The noodles should be firm.
2. Heat a cast iron or non-stick skillet over high heat and add 2 Tbsp of vegetable oil and a handful of noodles. Stir and separate the noodles with a chopstick, working them from the top to the bottom of the pan three times. Add pepper and salt to taste. Transfer to a serving dish. Repeat with the remainder of the noodles, adding more oil each time.
3. Stir-fry the pork butt and set aside. (A quick alternative is to use sliced char siu because it only needs to be warmed up.)
4. Stir-fry the vegetables slightly in the pan you used to cook the meat. They should be crispy. Mix them in with the meat.
5. The noodles must be dull and chewy for this dish. Fry them in a single batch one more time or top them with the meat and vegetables and place them in a preheated 350°F oven for 25 minutes.
6. To make the *kinshi tamago*, place the eggs, sugar, salt, oil, and dissolved cornstarch (if using) in a large bowl and mix together.
7. Lightly oil a square (or round) skillet and warm over medium heat.
8. Pour some of the egg mixture into the pan and cook on both sides. Remove from pan. Repeat with rest of egg mixture.
9. Let cool, cut into thin strips, and add to the top of the chow mein.
10. Add a sprinkle of *beni shoga* and *shoyu* soy sauce to taste.

10

Working Title

MATT RADER

The junior movie producer lived in a mid-century bungalow near the river. I knew the house because when I was a kid, on Wednesday nights before Catechism, we'd drop my dad there for a men's group.

The men's group was run by a big guy called Tenison. He was always standing on the paved walkway smoking when we pulled up. I knew him because he was friends with our neighbour, Marie. They'd sit out on Marie's deck most Friday evenings and drink beer and smoke. From my bedroom, I could hear them laughing.

When my dad was working a shutdown in a mill somewhere in the province, and Mum was on call, she'd gather us up early in the morning and deposit us at Marie's place. Marie always answered the door in a short yellow robe. My brother and I, perched at the kitchen bar, liked to watch her smooth calves flex and unflex as she made coffee.

Then Tenison would appear in the kitchen doorway like a weather event of unpredictable intensity. Or that's how we felt about him because that's how we felt about most men of considerable size. But he only ever said nice things and made us frybread.

The junior movie producer was a big guy too. There was a photo of him scaling a mountainous rockface on the dining room wall and another of him in climbing gear on top of a mountain. He was named Zephyr, but everyone called him Zeph.

He had his broad back to me making lattes on a machine in his kitchen, tamping espresso grounds into a filter. The kitchen was open to the dining room where I was standing looking at the photos.

He was talking about a blockchain project and Indigenous energy sovereignty. I wasn't sure how the two were connected. He fit the portafilter into the machine.

It's a black box, Zeph said about the blockchain scheme, that I can fill with content for potential investors.

The machine groaned and steamed and ran water through itself.

A digital black box secured by blockchain to protect Indigenous creators.

I intuited what he was saying without really understanding.

We'd known each other for about ten years already but this was the first time we'd gotten together to talk about movies.

Energy sovereignty is a great phrase, I said, just as he turned to hand me a clear mug of light brown coffee and milk.

Cheers, he said.

The furniture in the sunken living room was low and stylish. I sat in a tan leather chair the shape of a tea cup so low I could comfortably stretch my legs out on the parquet floor. I put the coffee cup on a glass side table.

Zeph sat perpendicular to me at one end of a teakwood and leather couch with his right arm across the back. In the middle of the room floated a surfboard coffee table on a faded Persian rug. The coffee table looked like walnut. The rug looked like a roiling sea.

I guess you'd call me a junior movie producer, he laughed. Movies was a new business for him.

I sent Stan your book of stories, Zeph said. He loved them. The Goodwin stuff. The striking coal miners. Gritty, poetic. He's been looking for the right treatment of the Goodwin story. What he wants to know is if there's more.

And Stan's an entertainment lawyer? I asked.

Do you listen to Graham Parker? the junior movie man said, leaping to his feet and padding over to the turntable in the opposite corner of the room. I texted you that I'd have Elvis Costello on, but then I was flipping through the vinyl, I remembered Parker.

The name sounds familiar, I said, but it's a familiar name.

He lowered the needle and something like an Elvis Costello song started humming from the two black speakers.

Yes, Zeph said, Stan's a lawyer and he's worked a lot of productions. Apparently, there's a golf cart with his name on it down at the Universal lot, Zeph laughed.

I pictured a small gold plate engraved with "Stan" affixed to the side of the cart. Then I wondered where such a cart might be parked all the days Stan wasn't riding around in it.

Everyone should have a monogrammed golf cart, I said.

I don't really know anything about movies, I said. About writing them I mean. But for years I told people I was working on a novel. What I was really doing was writing those stories, like feints and jabs at what a novel-sized story might be. I had an idea though. For a novel. About Goodwin, but also not about him. It would make a good movie. Or a series.

Have you seen *Pinky Blinders*? Zeph said.

I have, I said.

I love *Taboo* with Tom Hardy, Zeph said. I want to make something like that. I remember you telling me about Goodwin, about the novel, sitting in the Waverley one time. I think it was before they renovated.

I nodded. I used to think about the Number Six Mine pithead, I said. I don't know how deep that mine went, but it was just below the old firehall and village works yard across from the Waverley, so I always imagined we were drinking on top of some kind of history.

Yeah, Zeph said, I remember you saying that.

My idea spans ten years from 1911 to 1921. It has all these dimensions that are contemporary: energy security, environmental degradation, labour unrest, racial violence, global powers, war, a pandemic.

So, you're thinking a series, Zeph said.

I don't know, I said. You tell me.

When I moved back to Cumberland, I'd ride my bike over to the coffee shack at Dunsmuir and 4th with Melissa and the kids. There were always guys there who were either home from camp or heading out to camp. It was just after the recession and there were direct flights to the oil fields.

That's what got me thinking about labour, the history in Cumberland. Remembering my dad being away, I guess. He'd call from Quesnel or Chetwynd or wherever. He'd call collect, say his name to the operator so we'd know he was ok, then hang up so we didn't incur the charges.

Everyone I knew growing up in the valley had a dad who worked somewhere else. Fishing. Fixing helicopters. Working a shutdown on some giant pulp mill.

That's the thing about resource extraction, I said, you go away to do it. All those miners in Cumberland came from somewhere else. England. Northern Italy. China.

Zeph was nodding his head. What's the story though? What's the romance? Who's the bad guy? The Dunsmuirs?

The Dunsmuirs had already sold the mine by then.

Zeph looked off across the room like he was thinking. Out the window opposite me, I could see a little flash of the river framed by maple trees. The river drained the same lake where Goodwin was hiding in the summer of 1918. Seventy years later someone discovered the fossilized skeleton of an 80-million-year-old elasmosaur swimming in the rock of that very riverbed.

Look at this, I said, gesturing Zeph toward the lakeshore. The morning lakewater was dark and clear, the sky shimmering against the cold depths. Before us the earth rose into mountains populated by evergreens, the lake misting in the high-summer sun.

The opening shot is the lake from high above the treetops. The dark mirrored reflections of trees and sky.

The mountains so clear they ring.

1918 in big numerals. Like a stamp.

The camera moves out over the water and down the lake where a small boat is headed away from us to the far side, twin streams of light breaking in its wake.

In the forest below Alone Mountain, Albert Goodwin is dead. We see his corpse, already three days old, moldering in the dirt. Two men with rifles encamped around the body.

Then the camera moves towards the lake where a third armed man stands on the shore, waiting for the boat, now coming toward us, the growing whine of the motor.

Who are they? Zeph asked, as we watched the inspector step from the boat into a foot of lakewater.

The manhunters who were hired to track Goodwin down after he led a one-day walkout at the Trail smelter. First World War. The smelter made metals for the war effort.

Goodwin wanted an eight-hour workday. That was the demand. And for an end to the pollution. He wrote a letter about it. He describes the trees in the river valley as sickly and black. That's 1917. More than a hundred years ago already.

That's what got him drafted to the war? Zeph asked. Came all the way back to Vancouver Island and across Comox Lake to hide out?

But he wasn't the only one out here, I said, gesturing at the trees and the thimbleberry and the salal. There were other draft dodgers being fed and supplied by allies in Cumberland.

So, the movie begins with Goodwin dead?

The movie begins with Goodwin dead because the story isn't really about Albert Goodwin. It's about what happened before he was killed and what happened after. It's about what's happening right now.

What's happening right now?

Right now, I said, we're on a plane on the tarmac in Comox. You're an electrician headed for a stint at Syncrude. I'm a writer going back to my job at the university in Edmonton after visiting my family on Camp Road.

We're wearing face masks because that's the law. Out the thumbnail window, I can see the propeller, its five distinct blades, as it starts to turn.

Zeph shifts uncomfortably in his seat. These seats, he says, are so fucking small.

Down the aisle from us, a flight attendant is explaining to a man who doesn't speak English that he has to keep his mask on. Across the aisle, a woman with bright orange nails is talking on the phone, a blue mask dangling from her ear.

As the propeller begins to turn the five blades become many blades then one blade spinning then it disappears altogether and I can see through it to a woman in a safety vest with two orange cones in her hands, a white motorized cart stopped just behind her. The whole cabin vibrates with the sound and energy of the engines.

In the movie, I tell Zeph, when the inspector comes ashore the camera pans back, and we see the man with the rifle and the inspector disappear into the forest in the direction of the body.

That's when you get the title card.

And what's the title? Zeph asked, holding his coffee mug with two hands.

Someone will want to call it *Goodwin*, I imagine.

Maybe a little ironic.

I agree.

I wanted to call my novel *Working Title*.

What happens after the title card?

The film goes back in time to 1911.

Zeph nodded. So, he said, the mines are at full operation. The colliery port is bringing in ships from all over the world. The Chinese are building homes in the swampland.

Exactly, I said. It's a cosmopolitan place. You can buy bananas from a vine in the Union Bay store. Sun Yat-sen comes to raise money for the Chinese Republic. Mother Jones is photographed in Nanaimo rallying striking miners. Goodwin is working the coal seams.

It doesn't really matter the historical accuracy, I said. It's a movie. It's a black box we can fill with content for potential investors.

Zeph laughed. I know what Stan will say. He'll say, Sun Yat-sen and Mother Jones are lovers and they've arranged a secret rendezvous on Vancouver Island.

What I want to know, he said, is where the women are in this story. And you have these two watersheds, one here coming out of the Beaufort Range, and then the big Columbia River watershed, so dammed up it powers a whole corner of the continent.

Zeph had a way of flexing and unflexing his fingers as he spoke.

I'm thinking Sinixt, he said, K'ómoks. We'd need someone from those communities to consult.

Zeph was right. Here we were, two pale-skinned men sitting in Tenison's house doing our own men's group for the purposes of making money. Who was Tenison, I wondered, where was his home?

Zeph got up and went to the stereo to turn the record over. It was only then I realized the music had stopped.

The years I researched this story, I said, the hardest part to find details on was how people actually lived. What kinds of utensils they had, what kinds of meals they cooked, vegetables they grew. The insides of homes.

Women's work, Zeph said.

Exactly.

A space opened up then in Zeph's living room, a quality of being together and separate at the same time. I could tell Zeph felt it too. Who was missing. What was missing. Who could understand this conversation and who was excluded. It was the hard work of thinking too much and not thinking enough at the same time.

Then he put the needle down and a backbeat returned.

My story is about two young people, I told Zeph. One is the son of a miner. The other the daughter of a mine manager. They're twelve in 1911 at the beginning of the story and twenty-two at the end in 1921.

After the title card, we get a shot of Dunsmuir Avenue looking up the hill towards the lake, the street muddy with horseshit. 1911. I don't know how movie people make it look like it once did. Or what's possible. But that's the image in my mind. The hotels, the Big Store, wooden boardwalk. No one around.

Suddenly, a huge murmuration of starlings rises from the street like a big dark thought cloud.

I thought starlings came from Europe, Zeph said.

Yes, I said, that's part of the dark thought.

Zeph laughed. Okay, then what?

Maybe a wedding? Like *The Godfather*. Get everyone in the same place.

How about a union meeting? Zeph said.

Two meetings, I said. One union meeting where we see Goodwin in the crowd, not part of the union leadership yet. We see the boy standing at the back. Joe Naylor is talking. Maybe Mother Jones is there too but we don't know it's her yet. The way the camera moves we get the sense that the boy and Naylor are connected.

Joe Naylor?

He was the real union man. He's buried right next to Goodwin in the Cumberland cemetery. No headstone. Just a little plaque. He's a character through the whole story. The patriarch of the story, I guess. Goodwin's mentor.

I don't know why Naylor wasn't drafted, but he wasn't. I interviewed an old guy from Cumberland who knew Naylor. John would've been pretty young back then, but he told me Naylor had a wooden leg. That Naylor would pare an apple then stick the knife in the wooden thigh.

Put that in a movie, Zeph said.

The second meeting, I went on, is in the Chinese National League building. Sun Yat-sen is addressing the room. One white guy sitting at the front watching the faces of the crowd, trying to understand. Peering through a crack in the back door, behind where Sun is speaking, an eleven-year-old girl, glasses, hair pulled back, her first proper pimple swelling above her eye.

Just then Zeph's phone dinged and he looked down at the glowing screen on the table.

It's my daughter, he said, picking up the phone.

Sure, I said, looking out the window at the river. How many people have bathed in that river, I wondered, swam over the remains of ancient animals. It looked like a silver banner rippling between the trees.

I liked the song that was playing. The singer was admitting he did everything wrong.

She wants money, Zeph said.

How much?

Twenty. For gas.

Stan would say, Tell her you're very disappointed in her asking so little.

Zeph laughed then typed something with his thumbs.

There are three guys, he said like he could read my mind, who go down to the river there every morning, all year around, and bathe. Even in the winter they're down there just after sunrise. Two older men and a middle-aged guy. Young middle-age. Late 40s maybe. He's huge. Several inches taller than me. The two older guys arrive together in a green Tacoma. The big guy drives a silver Camry. He looks like a human pocket knife unfolding himself out of the car.

Ever talk to them?

No, Zeph said, it feels like a private thing. Ceremonial.

That's how I feel about history sometimes, like it's a private thing, like it's important to protect the privacy of lives lived before our own.

Like Goodwin's?

How old's your daughter now? I asked, Seventeen?

She'll be eighteen in a month.

That's how old the kids are in my story in 1917. The boy is just old enough to be drafted. That's how he ends up out there in the bush with Goodwin.

First there's the Great Strike. 1912-1914. The miners are dispossessed of their company homes. They set up a big camp in the mudflats at Royston. They don't have enough food. The Chinese in the swamplands are cut off from the rest of the community by Company men on horseback. Bombs. Shootings. The Seaforth Highlanders get their first deployment to Dunsmuir Avenue. Cannons up and down the street. That's the whole first act, the first series. 1911-1914.

Then the Great War. It wasn't popular among workers. No muleskinner wanted to charge across some muddy French field and try to kill another muleskinner.

Then the walkout in Trail, Zeph said, the year on the run, drinking the cold Cruikshank water out there on the far side of the lake.

Look at him, I said, pointing to the young man, knees to his chest behind an ancient cedar. He's trembling. He's a kid in an almost grown body with men hunting his comrades.

When they take Goodwin's body out of the woods and Naylor goes into the hotel parlour where it's laid out on a table like a map for men to puzzle over, all hell breaks loose. There's a huge funeral procession with a marching band all the way to the cemetery. There's the first general strike in Canadian history in Vancouver. Some boss gets thrown out a second story window.

Why was Goodwin so important though? Zeph asked. Why was there such a reaction?

He's not, I said. I already told you that. He's one of your black boxes. History is inscribed on his name.

That's poetic, Zeph said.

Goodwin was the writer, the storyteller. He wrote for newspapers. He wrote for the unions.

So, who tells the story when the storyteller is dead? Zeph asked.

Exactly, I said.

But here's the young man from the woods. The boy in the man's body from all those years ago at the union meeting. His beard as threadbare as his clothes. Nightfall. A small troupe of draft dodgers soft-shoeing down the backsteps of the hardware store.

And in the dimness of the basement, the girl with glasses from years before, womanly and clear-eyed, is cutting his hair and shaving him, and an older man is fitting him for clothes, trousers, vest, jacket. They're transformed and sent off into the world to tell a new story.

What's that story? Zeph asked.

That's series three, I said.

Zeph laughed, then his phone pinged. Then it pinged again twice in succession.

Series three, I said, involves a failure of conviction, a mutiny on a Canadian warship, a military expedition to Vladivostok, a long harrowing adventure across Russia back into Europe in the aftermath of the War.

Sounds expensive, Zeph said, glancing at this phone.

Look, I said, right now the plane is banking over Edmonton, getting ready to make its final descent. The flight attendants are coming down the aisle with plastic bags for our plastic cups and miniature wine bottles. The woman with the bright orange nails is rummaging in her handbag. They're telling her to put her tray table away.

I have another meeting, Zeph said, in fifteen. Stan is going to love this.

My dad used to come here, I said, for a men's group on Wednesday evenings. This same house.

So, how's it end? Zeph said.

With an elasmosaur raising its long neck out of the lake.

Seriously? Zeph said.

No.

It ends with the Spanish Flu and mask mandates. Our young woman wearing a linen face mask as she brings food to the doorsteps of infected houses. Her wiping the brow of the young man on a hospital cot, his fingers turning blue.

Grim, Zeph said.

Honestly, I don't know. It isn't written yet. But when I see her in my mind, calves flexing and unflexing as she moves from patient to patient, white shoreline of scalp, deep brown eyes behind two thick image-warping circles of glass, I begin to see all the people wearing masks on the bus in 2021. Hospital rooms with ventilators. Queues to enter the supermarket. Blue masks on the sidewalk.

I see black and white images of police riding on horseback into a crowd of striking miners. I see truncheons and bandanas and tear gas. Two young girls going hungry in the Royston mudflats. Temporary fencing and barricades. Dogs.

Someone is standing on top of a car throwing rocks. Someone is throwing blood on a painting.

Your daughter locking arms with my daughter and lying down in the middle of the street, ready to use their bodies to stop what is trying to kill them.

The ground rushing up to meet the plane until suddenly we come level and out the window, the world we'd left for a moment flashing by us all over again.

11

Tales from the Trail

ANDREW FINDLAY

It's hard not to feel a little nostalgic riding past the yellow gate and entering the labyrinth of trail that is the Cumberland network. It's short-sleeves weather. Trillium flowers are blossoming in the forests of Vancouver Island, while western toads croak their horny approval of spring's arrival. By 9:00 a.m. on this mid-week morning, the trailhead parking lot was already half-full. It's a testament to the fact that Cumberland's trail network—two hundred kilometres (124 miles) and counting, virtually all built on private forest land—is the fifth-most used network in North America. That's according to the popular Trailforks app, at least.

What a journey it's been.

"There are so many memories in these hills. A bridge here that I built with my girls, a berm there, a rock that we moved," says Jeremy Grasby, while out for a rip on trails he could almost navigate blindfolded.

A solo woman on an e-bike is paused at Sykes Bridge, studying her smartphone intensely.

"You all good? You know where you're going?" Grasby, the consummate trail ambassador, asks.

"I think so," she replies.

She'll figure it out. His embassy services only go so far. Especially on the first warm day of the season when an electric springtime buzz fills the air, the dirt is tacky, and the snowline has receded into the shady folds of the Beaufort Range.

To say that Cumberlanders are proud of their trails is like saying that Canadians like maple syrup. Civic pride built this trail network, and pride is written into the cultural DNA of Cumberland.

To understand where Cumberland is today, you need to understand where Cumberland was yesterday. In the late 1800s, prospectors discovered coal in these wild rolling hills ten kilometres (six miles) from the Salish Sea. Early attempts to mine these claims failed. Then along came Scottish wheeler and dealer Robert Dunsmuir.

At the time, Canada was a new—and incomplete—country. The colony of British Columbia, which included Vancouver Island, agreed to join the Dominion in 1871 on the condition that a railway be built to join "the seaboard of BC with the railway system of Canada." A decade of political turmoil in Ottawa delayed its construction. When Sir John A. Macdonald returned to power after a by-election in Victoria, he promised the terminus of the new railway would be in Esquimalt. The reward to the builder of the island railway would be $750,000 and 8,000 square kilometres (3,088 square miles) of land, the timber above ground, and all the minerals below it except the gold. In 1884, the shrewd Dunsmuir stepped up to claim this prize, which included the land on which Cumberland would eventually sprout. It was a massive grab and giveaway of Indigenous territory that would shape land use, development, and access on the east coast of Vancouver Island in profound ways.

Dunsmuir cared little about trains. He wanted the coal, a valuable commodity that would fuel industry around the world. The Dunsmuir family became the richest in the province, and Cumberland grew into a bustling, multicultural mining community populated by immigrants from across Europe and Asia. Workers of colour earned less than half the wage of whites, and the treacherous mines exacted a terrible toll on those who worked in them. More than three hundred workers perished in mining accidents and from related illnesses. The hardship of life working underground forged a labour movement and a deep community-minded spirit and solidarity that would shape the zeitgeist of Cumberland.

Then, when the last coal mine shut in the 1960s, Cumberland fell into a deep slumber that would last for decades. Wooden buildings fell into disrepair. The main street, Dunsmuir Avenue, was soon pocked with crater-sized potholes. Dunsmuir's private land empire had long since been parcelled up and sold to a number of timber companies. Now the biggest business in town was selling mugs of Lucky Lager and cigarettes at the Waverley Hotel and two other local bars. Non-residents sneered at the village, labelled it Scumberland. But for everyone who mocked it unfairly, someone recognized its organic grittiness and charismatic appeal. Cumberland had a fascinating story that echoed loudly despite the peeling paint. The fact that you could buy a fixer-upper heritage house for less than $80,000 also had a certain appeal for people like Grasby who were looking for affordable character.

In the late 1990s, Grasby worked for the BC Forest Service in Campbell River. He regularly drove to Cumberland to compete in local XC races on trails that have long since been consumed by a modern, decidedly generic-looking gentrified housing development on the village's outskirts some people now call Little Alberta. Back then there was a small but well-established trail-building and riding scene. It was a rogue enterprise—carving out trails on private forest land. The ethic of the day was "build first and ask for permission later."

ABOVE The Riding Fool Hostel opening event was co-organized with Dodge City Cycles. With the Village of Cumberland's permission a few loads of dirt were trucked in to create jump piles for locals. COURTESY OF JEREMY GRASBY

"It was grassroots. I felt right at home," Grasby says, recalling those early days.

However, life took him elsewhere for a time. He had applied for, and been offered, another forestry job—in Merritt, a ranching and logging town south of Kamloops—while working in Campbell River.

"The worst decision of my life," he says.

By then Vancouver Island, and Cumberland in particular, had sunk its incisors into his soul. He started scratching out an exit plan on the back of a napkin to open a mountain biking-friendly hostel in Cumberland. He quit his government job, took a small severance payout, cashed in his meagre retirement benefits, and moved to Cumberland to execute his plan.

ABOVE After seven months of renovations to the historic Tarbell's hardware store, the Riding Fool Hostel opened its doors in the spring of 2003. A ribbon-cutting ceremony was held, and the then Mayor Fred Bates cut the ribbon. COURTESY OF JEREMY GRASBY

The Riding Fool Hostel opened in 2003 in a 120-year-old former hardware store that was a windows-smashed-out shell of a building before Grasby and a small army of friends and volunteers undertook what turned into a seven-month renovation. To celebrate the opening, Grasby phoned the village office to ask if they could dump a few truckloads of dirt on Dunsmuir Avenue and build jumps. They said "Yes."

Soon after, he began to divert some energy to local trail building, following in the footsteps of the likes of Dan Espeseth (now the long-time owner of Dodge City Cycles), James Powsey (before he became a tugboat captain), Jeff "Jefe" Guerney, and too many other local folks bound by bikes doing what they love to do—building trails and riding them—to mention. They would camp out overnight on the hills above town to work on trails like Grub & Stub. Closer to town, there were wiggly single-tracks like Black Hole, named after an old, collapsed coal shaft hidden in the bush next to the trail.

Grasby and some of his trail-building buddies took to calling themselves THC—the Trail Harvesting Club. And harvest they did. The network grew in a sort of organized anarchy, the way mycelium spread beneath the forest floor and manifest magically as mushrooms. And so did the popularity of trails like Steam Donkey and Teapot, named after historical artifacts found in the woods, and Crafty Butcher, a name that emerged from one of the builders' off-colour sense of humour. Cumberland was morphing organically from a local trail secret into a 100 per cent, volunteer-built destination for riding.

TimberWest and Island Timberlands, the two companies that owned most of the land around Cumberland, had so far tolerated, and at times even assisted, trail-building efforts. But it was a tenuous relationship. Besides community goodwill, there wasn't much upside to allowing recreation on their lands—just risk. Risk of forest fire, the annoyance of riders and trail builders impeding logging operations, and the potential liability if someone broke their neck while sending a jump on Bucket of Blood, a trail that marked a turning point in the evolution of Cumberland's trail network.

A group of five riders is munching trail snacks at the rocky knoll where Bear Buns and Bucket of Blood start. The latter is an original Cumberland classic. It has rock rolls, janky off-camber roots, drops, and spicy wooden features. And it's gone through many evolutions and iterations. When it was first built, the trail descended entirely through mature second-growth forest. Now it weaves in and out of young and old trees.

In 2008, when local riders got word that TimberWest was planning to log Bucket of Blood, it sparked panic. The logging company had made it clear that nothing could be done to legitimize trails on their land before there was a land use agreement in place. Ninety-six per cent of British Columbia is public land, or Crown land—a holdover from the days of British colonization. There are procedures, laws, and protocols in place for developing recreational trails on public lands—an entire government agency is dedicated to overseeing them. In this sense, Cumberland, being surrounded by private land, is an anomaly, and it makes for unique challenges. There was no road map for negotiating land use agreements with a private corporation, but something had to be done to formalize mountain biking's relationship with its de facto landlords. Otherwise its future was uncertain, possibly even doomed.

Concern about losing Bucket of Blood prompted Grasby and Colin Wilson, a chiropractor and fellow mountain-biking enthusiast, to organize a meeting with local politicians to make the case for mountain biking's economic, social, and community benefits. In a stroke of genius, Wilson made a digital map with two layers, one showing all the trails and the other showing all the officially sanctioned trails around Cumberland. The former was a spider's web of wiggly lines; the latter was more or less blank. It was a compelling graphic, but when the duo made their plea for help in developing a land use agreement, one of the politicians asked, "Who are you, and who do you represent?"

"That's when we knew we had to get our shit together," Grasby recalls.

So they did. By that time, they were informally calling themselves UROC (United Riders of Cumberland). But in December of 2008, UROC officially incorporated as a society. Its inaugural five-member board included Grasby as president and Mike Manara as treasurer, and they would play a key role in checking off item #2 on the society's nine-item constitution: to foster a positive working relationship with landowners to facilitate land access.

One of the first bylaws the UROC board established to guide meetings read as follows: "Beer: late guy buys beer unless arriving before 9:00 p.m."

It would take a lot of beer, scrutinizing of maps, and talking to foresters to achieve the next major milestone. In 2015, UROC signed a land use agreement with the logging companies that covered twenty-six square kilometres (6,500 acres) of working forest. The agreement dealt with the liability question and with a stroke of the pen legitimized a trail network that had outgrown its renegade origins. It was a pioneering agreement. Official trail signage and map kiosks could now be built. UROC—and Cumberland—could market the trails and confidently apply for grants to pay for trail maintenance and trail crew, something funders wouldn't have touched with a ten-foot pole when the network was unsanctioned.

Gone were the days of free-for-all trail building. At first UROC got pushback from some people who had grown accustomed to building wherever and whenever they wanted. But on the plus side, there was now a formal process in place for cooperative dialogue with the logging companies to get new trails approved. In turn, the companies agreed to share their logging plans with UROC.

Up high in the network, Dougal Browne and his crew were scratching out a trail linking the bottom of Racerocks with Potluck, so named when the original trail builders stumbled across an illicit outdoor cannabis grow-op in the woods.

"This trail makes for a continuous black diamond single-track descent from the top of the network at 720 metres to the trail-head," says Browne, who signed on as UROC's first full-time executive director in 2019.

It's a busy role. Browne looks after UROC's full-time trail crew of three, as well as eleven other builders who are contracted on a project-by-project basis. He manages the land use agreement with the logging companies and works closely with Cumberland Community Forest Society, which has bought and preserved more than two square kilometres (more than five hundred acres) of forest land next to the village (some of Cumberland's oldest and most beloved close-to-town trails like Space Nugget and Orange

Peels lie within the Community Forest). On top of this, Browne fills out funding grant applications and massages relationships between the growing numbers of trail runners, hikers, and dog walkers who share the trails with the mountain bikers.

However, he's happiest when he has dirt under his fingernails. When Browne talks trail he gets a feverish look of excitement in his eyes. He loves trails—planning them, building them, riding them, watching other people enjoy them.

How Browne ended up managing one of the busiest trail networks in North America is somewhat random. His accent is ambiguous, reflective of an international upbringing as the son of a Scottish-born, British military father who bounced around from posting to posting with his family. In 2008, while living in South Africa, he met his Canadian future wife in a bar. And that is how he eventually ended up living in Bowser, a small seaside community south of Cumberland. Freelancing as a surfboard importer gave him plenty of time to pursue his volunteer trail-building passion at a place called Cook Creek.

"Trails are like art. Seeing a forest, a piece of land, and imagining what it could be," he says.

Cook Creek was a time-consuming, non-paying obsession that he had to convince his wife would eventually pay off. He just didn't know how. When UROC advertised for the executive director position, he applied for what sounded like—and has turned out to be—the perfect job for a trail obsessive.

"I have a degree in construction management and town planning, so I guess I'm using my education," Browne says with a chuckle.

No sooner had Browne stepped into his role with UROC than COVID-19 dropped like a bomb. After the initial shock of the pandemic shutdown, there was an unexpected explosion in interest in mountain biking. From seven-year-olds to seventy-year-olds, from plumbers to pediatricians, and every demographic you can imagine, everyone seemed to be suddenly looking to ride blue square flow trails.

Browne has an accountant's fondness for numbers. Before the pandemic, nine trail counters in the Cumberland network recorded 120,000 trail rides. In 2022, they recorded 220,000.

"Trailforks captures kilometres travelled for each user and the Cumberland average ride is seventeen kilometres," Bowne says, before doing the math. "It's like Cumberland riders are pedalling the equivalent of crossing Canada 368 times in a year. It's a fairly loose statistic, but a fun one nonetheless."

The simple takeaway is that Cumberland trails are popular and well used. What also became clear during the pandemic is that Cumberland had long since outgrown the Scumberland stigma of the past. More and more people were cashing out and fleeing places like Vancouver and moving to Cumberland. In 2021, long-time locals were shocked when a renovated mining shack on Camp Road sold for $1 million. Proximity to trails was proving to be a big draw for newcomers.

"We've been working bollocks on trails for the past few years," says Browne, explaining that his five-year vision is to grow the network to the full capacity of the land use agreement at an elevation of 980 metres (3,200 feet).

Success at trail stewardship had helped create a different kind of success—more than big commissions for real estate agents. Cumberland had become a brand unto itself. Twenty years ago, people would go to the red brick government building to collect their mail. Now they go there to buy vinyl from the hipster Moon's Records. On sunny afternoons, a few hundred thousand dollars' worth of mountain bikes could be chained up outside Cumberland Brewing Company, where the outdoor patio is frequently jammed with post-ride cheer. It's the same story at the legendary Waverley Hotel.

In 2018, British-born Owen Pemberton, a design engineer at Norco Bicycles at the time, eyed up Cumberland as the place to launch his start-up brand, Forbidden Bike Company.

"Right from the beginning my goal was to have a bike company that was integrated into a bike culture," Pemberton says from Forbidden Bike Company's office and warehouse, which are tucked behind Beaufort Cycles, a bike shop near the entrance to Cumberland. "We can go for lunch-hour company rides. When I was at Norco we didn't do that because we were an hour's drive from the trailhead."

These are busy days for the brand. Forbidden just dropped the Druid II onto the market and has forged a bike demo partnership with Gravity MTB, a mountain bike coaching company that recently opened a training centre called Gravity Garage next to a cannabis retailer. Early in 2023, Forbidden signed homegrown, nineteen-year-old Enduro phenom Emmy Lan, who took top honours in last year's U-21 Enduro World Series. Although Lan lives nearby in Comox, Cumberland is like her second home. Lan started riding mountain bikes on Cumberland dirt at age seven—and she's in good company. This network has spawned no shortage of shredders, including the veteran, well-decorated Olympian and Canadian national XC champ Geoff Kabush, Giant Factory rider Carter Woods, and cyclecross and XC crusher Emilly Johnston, who recently signed with Trek Future Racing.

For Lan, joining a local brand is a dream come true.

"It's sick to have Forbidden [Bike Co.] fifteen minutes from where I live," she says. "Growing up riding in Cumberland is a big reason for my success. These trails have their own kind of jank. When I want to train in the off season, I don't need to go anywhere else."

Equally important in her development as a rider, she says, is being surrounded by such a strong biking community and local athletes to look up to, like Johnston and Woods.

Forbidden is not alone in seeing the branding and cycling lifestyle potential of Cumberland. In the spring of 2023, NOBL Wheels relocated to a renovated Dunsmuir Avenue heritage building that once housed a consignment clothing store, among many other enterprises in its hundred-year history.

When NOBL owner Trevor Howard was thinking about moving shop from Langley, a suburb of Vancouver, Squamish and

Pemberton were on the list at first. But the numbers didn't make sense. Vancouver Island, and specifically Cumberland, seemed like the logical choice.

"Trevor always wanted NOBL to be part of a cycling-centred community," says Chris Arruda, NOBL's operations manager. "Everybody is stoked to be here."

Add to this mix the long-running bike store Dodge City Cycles and more recent arrival Beaufort Cycles, as well as guiding company Island Mountain Rides, and it's safe to say that Cumberland has a cycling economy.

Dougal Browne calls it "a bike industry shift" toward Cumberland. "I'm always blowing smoke up the trail builders because they're the ones who got it all going," he says.

He's right. The numbers say it all. In 2004, Cumberland had eleven trails. Today it has two hundred. But sometimes the classics draw you back, the way a song from days past can conjure up fond memories—a first date, a tailgater after an unforgettable ride.

Near the end of his ride, Jeremy Grasby stops to inspect recent trail maintenance that he did on Off Broadway with one of his two daughters. Then he ducks into Short N Curly. In the early days of the Riding Fool Hostel, when Grasby and Mike Manara were home-brewing thirty gallons of beer a year, a visitor jokingly told them to make sure not to get any "short 'n' curlies" in their batch.

"We thought, 'What a great trail name,'" he says, fondly recalling the naming of a trail he helped build and has ridden countless times.

Light flickers through the cedar and hemlocks. The tap of a pileated woodpecker echoes through the woods as Grasby negotiates roots and rocks that are seared into his muscle memory. Every trail has a story behind it, just as every mountain biking community has a tale to tell. Cumberland's just seems to get more and more interesting.

I ask Grasby if he ever envisioned what could be when he first opened the hostel with fingers crossed. "Fuck no," he says, laughing. "I was just buying myself a job so I could ride bikes and build trails." There's a long pause, then he asks, "By the way, who else are you interviewing for this story? I'm just one of many."

Indeed. They say it takes a community to raise a child. In Cumberland it took a community to build mountain-biking culture.

I walked out of
that forest
and into another story

SUSAN MUSGRAVE, *THE WOLF*

12

Welcome Poles

Home, Homelands, and Whose Land Is It Anyways?

GRANT SHILLING

In 2005, my family and I moved to Cumberland. We loved the "heritage" here and bought a 1905 Bevan* house: our first home after a life of renting. Cumberland was affordable for two artists with low incomes and a child. Our mortgage of $515 per month was $200 less than we were paying in rent on Salt Spring Island at the time.

I remember going to buy house insurance on the dubiously named Dunsmuir Avenue and the agent saying to me, "You better get used to people saying to you, 'That's because you're not from here.'"

Which begged the question, *who is* "from here"? At the time I saw no visible evidence that Cumberland was part of the "unceded territory of K'ómoks First Nation," and I'm really not sure that's who the agent was referring to.

---

* A Bevan house is one that was relocated from the former mining town of Bevan. The simple homes with distinct sloped roofs were cut in half, transported via rail, and reassembled in Cumberland.

Fast-forward to 2023. Cumberland is no longer affordable. Who is "from here" is even more contested. And "unceded territory" and "reconciliation" are a part of everyone's vocabulary. And yet . . .

For twelve years, I worked with the unhoused in the Comox Valley as an outreach worker for Dawn to Dawn Action on Homelessness Society (D2D). For nine of those years I have advocated and participated in an affordable housing development project called Ḱ̠wax̠dzi'dzas.

This project was initiated after my discussions with former Cumberland Mayor Leslie Baird made it clear that the land surrounding Cumberland Lodge was to be deeded back to the Village of Cumberland if a health care unit was not built on the site.

Baird found the long-lost deed. Cumberland Council agreed to lease the land to D2D to build affordable family housing. It took two years of trying before we could bring Island Health to the table. In the meantime, D2D and their new partner, Comox Valley Transition Society (CVTS) hired a consultant and plans began for a twenty-two-unit affordable family housing project in the increasingly unaffordable village of Cumberland.

Council agreed the land should be used for affordable housing. The community was engaged. BC Housing (BCH) noted that the community was more supportive of a project like this than any other community they had encountered.

What could go wrong?

In 2019, we thought we were there. After all, we had land! Not ours—it was unceded K'ómoks land—but still, it was the critical component in any BCH application. Our consultants were convinced it was a slam dunk.

Secure in this feeling, I applied for a BC Arts Council community development grant for the housing site with the goal of running Indigenous programming.

Here's the deal: Vancouver Island's population is almost 8 percent Indigenous, according to 2021 Census data, but various estimates suggest up to 40 percent of the unhoused population identifies as Indigenous. How can this happen to a people on their own lands?

The goal of K̓wax̱dzi'dzas since its inception has been to have a minimum of 40 percent Indigenous occupants and to have the design and management style reflect Indigenous values.

Well, long story short, BC Housing didn't provide the funding for K̓wax̱dzi'dzas. Apparently, it was unclear who the land belonged to on the unceded territory of K'ómoks First Nation (KFN). Island Health wasn't relinquishing the land that the Village wanted to lease to D2D.

In the meantime, D2D received the community development grant from the BC Arts Council for a series of workshops to create two welcome poles for the K̓wax̱dzi'dzas site. In the absence of funding for the housing, a call to BC Arts was in order. I fully expected to have to make a case as to why I felt we should proceed with the workshops nevertheless.

The BC Arts officer was completely understanding. "That's okay, Grant. Indigenization should come first."

If any level of government should be understanding, I had hoped it would be in the arts. I wasn't disappointed.

We held a series of well-attended workshops for the public at the Abbey in Cumberland, including cedar weaving, beading, and talks on two spiritedness, native plants, cultural safety, and protocol.

A five-hundred-year-old red cedar log from Kelsey Bay, the traditional unceded territory of Liǧwiłdax̌w and KFN, was gifted by Western Forest Products and delivered to the K̓wax̱dzi'dzas site.

Through the fall of 2022 and into 2023, Karver Everson of K'ómoks First Nation and Wei Wai Kum carver Junior Henderson worked on the stunning poles on the future K̓wax̱dzi'dzas site. In October 2022, a community potluck was held in Cumberland at the Cultural Centre to start the project off in a good way.

Over a hundred people joined Karver, Junior, numerous Elders, and the Kumugwe Cultural Society in a beautiful night of celebration.

Once the winter weather set in, the poles were moved into the gym of the Cumberland Community School. Students were given the opportunity to watch the poles being carved and to engage with the two artists.

"It's the most welcome I ever felt in Cumberland," said Karver.

With the poles close to completion and the Ḱ̲wax̱dzi'dzas housing not yet granted, the poles seemed destined to be wrapped in tarps and put in storage—a metaphor for government inaction on housing and hollow words of reconciliation.

But wait . . . After discussions with Karver and Junior, we decided to present to Council a proposal to put the poles up in an alternative location. Both the stunning beauty of the welcome poles and concerns about how long it would take BCH to actually grant the funding led to this decision. Once the funding was granted and the housing built, the poles would be moved to the Ḱ̲wax̱dzi'dzas site. We would apply for additional funding for poles to replace those that would be moved.

Council was most receptive to the idea. Several potential locations were discussed. Ultimately Karver, in discussion with Hereditary Chiefs, was to make the final decision.

In the meantime, discussions between the Village and Island Health continued. Many legal billing hours passed. Paperwork piled up on the unceded territory of K'ómoks First Nation. The Village of Cumberland and Island Health eventually reached an agreement. It was a done deal! No, wait . . . A date on the cover letter was wrong—lawyers and three weeks later it was corrected. Which makes me wonder, whatever happened to white out? And I'm not speaking metaphorically.

Karver and the Elders decided Cumberland Peace Park would be the most visible location for the welcome poles. Hereditary Kwakwa̱ka̱'wakw Chief Wedlidi Speck also noted that the park was a joint project between First Nations and members of the Bahá'i Faith who had reached out to Hereditary Chiefs about a collaborative project. "We've done several of them with the Bahá'i folks," says Wedlidi, "including one on Denman."

The park seemed like a natural fit. Eventually a roundabout will be constructed in the park due to an increase in traffic coming from the Coal Valley Estates subdivision. Current estimates are that this is at least three years away. The replacement poles will then be placed at the centre of the roundabout.

So, what is the significance of totem poles in the Valley?

"The biggest thing, the most important thing, is truth-telling," says Hereditary Chief Nagedzi (Rob Everson) of the Gilal'gam 'Walas Kwagu'l. "It's a matter of setting the record straight and stopping the perpetual erasure of our history." Chief Nagedzi offers what was once known as Pentlatch Lake as an example. "If they were to drain the lake, they would find village sites that existed into the 1800s at the mouth of the Cruickshank and Puntledge. It was all submerged with the dam and now it's known as Comox Lake, which is an erasure."

This erasure of history was hard to ignore when Vancouver Island's largest earthquake (and Canada's largest onshore earthquake ever recorded), with a magnitude of 7.3, happened on the Forbidden Plateau on June 23, 1946.

After the earthquake, hundreds of wooden stakes popped up out of the mud in the tidal zone of the Courtenay River Estuary, like witnesses to history. At one time, the poles were part of an intricate fish trap system created by the Pentlatch peoples, whose descendants are now part of KFN. Archeological surveys to this point mapped three hundred interconnected traps. These fish traps were built over at least thirteen hundred years and used as many as 200,000 hemlock and fir stakes.

Originally, there were an estimated three thousand Pentlatch people with ninety settlements in this region. The smallpox epidemic, a result of contact with Europeans, decimated those populations. By the 1930s the Pentlatch population had been reduced to two families at a village site at the mouth of the Courtenay River Estuary, which through the *Indian Act* came to be called Comox Indian Reserve Number One. The last fluent speaker of the Pentlatch language, Joe Nimnim, died in 1940, and Pentlatch was considered a "sleeping language." It is now considered a living language thanks to work by two semi-speakers, Qualicum First Nation Elder Bill Recalma and his son Jessie Recalma. About twenty others are also learning the language through a revitalization project. The Pentlatch hosted a ceremony celebrating the language's official reawakening in 2023.

In 1886, the famed anthropologist Franz Boas spent time among the K'ómoks interviewing people at the village. "It is the saddest-looking village I have seen," Boas wrote. "It is apparent that the inhabitants are dying out rapidly. There are ruins everywhere, and beautifully carved totem poles stand in front of empty shells."

His comments were made a year after the government's notorious ban on Potlatches in 1885. The ban was lifted in 1951. Legendary carver Mungo Martin would host the first legal Potlatch following the lifting of the ban. The poles at Lewis Park were originally carved by Mungo Martin in 1956 and raised in a traditional ceremony by K'ómoks Chief Andy Frank. These poles were replicated in 2002 by Calvin Hunt, Mungo Martin's step-grandson.

Totem poles now stand not in "front of empty shells" but at numerous locations in the Comox Valley. In 2014, when Chief Nagedzi was an Elected Chief with KFN, he set a goal of creating two Guardian poles a year. The K'ómoks First Nation Administration built poles carved by Karver Everson and Randy Frank under the mentorship of Calvin Hunt that same year. The poles reflect the four of the formerly separate Nations that make up KFN today, which are Pentlatch, Sahtloot, Ieeksen, and Sasitla.

Numerous poles followed at Courtenay Elementary School, Comox Marine Park, the front of the I-HOS gallery, and the Puntledge RV Campground. There are poles made by Karver Everson and Randy Frank on Denman and Hornby and at the Courtenay Airpark.

"Not only are Guardian poles markers of unceded territory," wrote Roger Albert, "they also exemplify the stories and belief systems that have been in place since time immemorial. They aim to uplift the spirits of the K'ómoks people and are also a means of educating non-Indigenous people about K'ómoks traditions and values."

The welcome poles for the Ḱ̲wax̲dzi'dzas site are the first in Cumberland.

With the go-ahead for the welcome poles to be installed at the Cumberland Peace Park, we set up a meeting with LaCasse Construction, which was contracted to install the poles, and the Village, Chief Nagedzi, and Karver Everson. A site was agreed upon, and everyone was pretty stoked for a big celebration on June 21, National Indigenous Peoples Day (NIPD).

What could go wrong?

Shortly after our meeting we received a message from the Village. Could we schedule the raising for another day? Another event was already scheduled on National Indigenous Day by Kómoks First Nation.

"National Indigenous Peoples Day does not belong to one band. There can be as many celebrations of the event as Indigenous people desire. K'ómoks First Nation does not own NIPD. If we want to celebrate that day, we will," Nagedzi said in response.

The Village was trying to be sensitive to everybody, but found itself caught between the elected Chief and Council and the Hereditary Chiefs.

"This situation allows for a teachable moment," said Nagedzi optimistically. "Many in the non-Indigenous community are trying to do the right thing, to walk humbly, to listen and learn." What is the "right thing" is sometimes slippery for us non-Indigenous folks to apprehend.

Elected Council and Chiefs were put in place through the *Indian Act* in 1876. They generally hold authority over reserve lands and infrastructure and are elected through a democratic vote by band members. The Chief and Council are employees of the federal government.

Elected Councils and Chiefs were implemented by the federal government of 1876 as a more familiar (that is, more familiar to the colonizers) way for them to deal with Indigenous communities.

"This policy," says Nagedzi, who is a Hereditary Chief and former elected Chief, "set out to eradicate the concept of Hereditary Chiefs, something that a western democracy did not understand."

Nagedzi said he feels elected councils have their place, which is dealing with on-reserve issues. "Their jurisdiction does not extend beyond the reserve," says Nagedzi. "That is the role of Hereditary Chiefs."

Hereditary Chiefs predate the imposed colonial law that created band councils. The roles of a Hereditary Chief are varied, explained Nagedzi. They differ between communities but mainly include leadership, territory, and traditional territories—land outside the reserve.

A meeting was scheduled to discuss when the celebration of raising the welcome poles would take place.

WHEN OUR FAMILY first looked to purchase our house in Cumberland I walked into the backyard. At the back was an old picket fence. Beyond the fence was this green space, which was grassed and lush with wildflowers, lupine, and foxglove. It was like a dream space of being. An alley commons. This space would become a place for my son, Levon, and his neighbouring friends to run wild. It belonged to everyone and no one. It was ours to share.

Early after we moved to Cumberland, my neighbour Andrew approached us about supporting the Cumberland Community Forest Society, which we did as best we could. It was so impressive that a community—then still lower-income and working-class—had created such a project. Community commons on a grander scale.

Shortly after moving to Cumberland we volunteered at the first ever Big Time Out, a music festival featuring Michael Franti from Spearhead. It seemed inconceivable such a headliner would come to such a relatively remote and still off-the-grid location.

Once a year the circus would come to town. Dunsmuir—a street that at one time you could shoot a cannon down without anyone noticing—would come alive.

Then a microbrewery. And by increments things changed. Then the pandemic came and the changes happened in leaps and bounds.

"The thing about Cumberland," one councillor told me, "was we did too many things right and the money and the people followed. In a way we are the victim of our own success."

Once set up in Cumberland, Levon and I walked to school together each day. Hand in hand we arrived. He'd give me a kiss and head for kindergarten. At the end of the day we would often walk through a wooded area behind the school. One day when we went it was blocked off—logging was in progress. The area was being cleared to make room for a developer's dream.

One weekend I went there to take pictures of the huge slash piles to document a changing Cumberland. Near where Levon and I used to walk I found a wood sign marked "Trail" in white block letters.

Blasting, a lot of blasting, followed.

Levon and I continued to walk the side streets to Cumberland Elementary (as it was called then). He no longer gave me a kiss—it was embarrassing for my growing boy—and eventually didn't hug me, and then he wanted to go to school on his own. The progress of love.

The area behind the school rapidly developed, as huge houses on sketchy slopes filled up the Kendall Road area. Honestly, the area was not part of our daily "reality." We lived in what was becoming a Potemkin Village in the confines of the original six or seven streets that surrounded Dunsmuir.

I have no doubts that the people on Kendall were no less happy than or any different from us.

Eventually Levon's mother and I divorced. The progress of love. Our Maryport home was sold to a family from Kendall who were nervous about the amount of traffic on their street and their children's safety.

Levon and I moved to a townhouse in a quiet cul-de-sac near the "poop loop," as the sewage treatment outfall area is affectionately called. My connection to Cumberland became defined by my time spent in the woods. The woods had become a lot busier.

RIGHT DługwayaX̱alis (Karver Everson) speaks about the process of creating the welcome poles and the opportunity to collaborate and learn from mentor Aaqwasgem (Junior Henderson), during an event in Cumberland's Peace Park on National Indigenous People's Day, June 21, 2023.
COURTESY OF JIM WHYTE

They needed to be managed. Challenges arose between hikers, bikers, and flying the old school Cumberland flag, ATV riders. Heck, some of the bikes cost as much as the down payment on our home.

All else around me was changing. This included our collective awareness of Indigenous issues and that word "reconciliation."

Yet the forces that displaced Indigenous people—the endless wheel of capitalism, colonialism, and an emphasis on growth—have us all in a hammerlock. The system is broken. The unhoused population continues to climb.

We banned the Potlatch and sanctified money.

ABOVE Cumberland community members gathered to witness and celebrate the raising of the poles.
COURTESY OF JIM WHYTE

Cumberland, a place that once had a systemic self-esteem problem, has a new pride in itself. The place we moved to because it was affordable is no more. This change is not limited to Cumberland but is an Island-wide trend.

Listen, let there be no doubt that I loved Cumberland and what it provided for my family. But what I had, I wish for others of modest means. And that is no longer achievable.

What we are doing—chasing constant growth—is not working. It's hard to be economically inclusive in a capitalist society. We still need what Joe Naylor and Ginger Goodwin fought for. Ḱ̠wax̠dzi'dzas will be a win for those families fortunate enough to find a home there. May there be more models like it—and may they not take nine years and counting to accomplish.

After discussions between the Village and Hereditary Chiefs, the pole-raising ceremony was held as planned on NIPD. It was a beautiful community celebration. Hereditary Chiefs, elected KFN councillors, Elders, wise women, and knowledge keepers attended. Over three hundred school children from Cumberland Community School who had witnessed the carving of the poles in their gym were present. It was a magical and historic day.

ABOVE The welcome poles in Peace Park. They will be relocated to the K̓wax̱dzi'dzas Cumberland Affordable Housing Project upon its completion, and new poles will be commissioned for Peace Park.
COURTESY OF JIM WHYTE

While we work collectively to ensure Indigenous history is no longer erased, I do wonder what the future will look like. And as traffic pours out of what once was a forest, the poles on the future roundabout will ring with the increasing noise of cars, where the road divides.

SOURCES

ALBERT, ROGER. "Standing Tall." *Collective Magazines*, Volume 16 (Fall). https://thecollectivemags.ca/3639847-2/

GLAVIN, TERRY. "A Lost World Returns." *Macleans*, November 2020. https://macleans.ca/news/human-remains-found-on-vancouver-island-have-opened-a-door-into-a-lost-world/

INDIGENOUS CORPORATE TRAINING INC. https://ictinc.ca

MUSGRAVE, SUSAN. *Tarts and Muggers*. Toronto, BC: McClelland and Stewart, 1982.

Contributors

RHONDA BAILEY has had a career as an editor, publisher, and teacher of publishing. She has worked as an editor for publishers across the country, served on the boards of national publishing associations, and holds a Master of Publishing degree from Simon Fraser University. Retired from the Creative Writing Department of Vancouver Island University, she is currently a VIU honorary research associate. Although deeply rooted in Nanaimo, Bailey feels connected to Cumberland through her family heritage: her maternal grandmother emigrated from Maryport in Cumberland, England, to Canada after the First World War, and two of her great-uncles worked in Vancouver Island coal mines. She was pleased to team up with the writers and the Cumberland Museum & Archives to develop this book.

TRACI SKUCE lived in Cumberland for over twenty years and now lives (not far away) in Courtenay. Her heart, though, remains in the Cumberland Community Forest. Traci's work has appeared in several literary journals throughout North America. In April 2020, her short story collection, *Hunger Moon*, was released by NeWest Press and was a finalist for the Rakuten Kobo Emerging Writer Prize. She is currently working on a novel that examines relationships in this time of climate crisis.

LYNNE BOWEN has a master's degree in Western Canadian History from the University of Victoria. She has written seven books of popular history, which have won several awards, including the Lieutenant Governor's Medal for Writing British Columbia

History, the Hubert Evans Nonfiction Prize, and the F.G Bressani Literary Prize for Creative Nonfiction. She taught creative writing at the University of British Columbia for fourteen years. She is married, has three children and three grandchildren, and has lived in Nanaimo since 1972.

KIM BANNERMAN writes novels and short stories from her home in Cumberland, BC. After receiving a BA in Anthropology from UBC, she completed further studies at the London School of Journalism while working as a promotional writer. Her essays have appeared in anthologies like *She's Shameless* from St. Martin's Press, *In the Company of Animals* from Nimbus Press, and *When Birds Are Near* from Cornell University Press. She received a Canada Council Grant to complete her historical murder mystery, *Bucket of Blood*. She is the author of twelve novels, including the Circus Salmagundi Mysteries series and a modern fairy tale, *The Tattooed Wolf*.

ROD MICKLEBURGH was a journalist for more than forty years, including twenty-three with the *Globe and Mail*. A co-winner of the Michener Award for coverage of Canada's tainted blood scandal, he was the *Globe*'s Beijing Bureau Chief from 1994 until 1998. With Geoff Meggs, he co-authored *The Art of the Impossible*, an entertaining account of BC's first NDP government under Dave Barrett, which won the BC Book Prize for nonfiction. Before joining the *Globe*, Rod was a labour reporter in Vancouver for sixteen years, and labour remains dear to his heart. *On the Line*, his definitive history of the BC labour movement, won the George Ryga Award for Social Awareness in Literature. He continues to work closely with the BC Labour Heritage Centre, hosting a regular podcast on the province's rich labour past.

DAVE FLAWSE writes at the intersection of history, science, and local interest for a selection of BC magazines. He is regularly published in the *British Columbia Review* with analyses of Canadian literature and is the publisher of VancouverIslandHistory.com, where readers discover the Island's unexpected past. A recipient of four publishing and writing awards, Dave achieved a Creative Writing degree from Vancouver Island University, where he was the managing editor of the literary magazine *Portal*. As a free-lance editor, he coaches writers to achieve their publication goals.

BEVIN CLEMPSON works in school libraries full-time and moon-lights as a copyeditor, copywriter, and writer. When not working on creative projects, you can find her walking streets, forests, and beaches with her dog, getting her kids to and from all sorts of places, dreaming up travel plans, or curled up with a book.

DR. TOM L.Q. WONG was born in Cumberland's Chinatown in 1930. After high school, he undertook auto mechanics training at the Dominion Provincial Training School, which he completed in 1950. He moved to Vancouver for his apprenticeship at Vancouver Motors, where he continued to work as he began his university studies. He received his BSc from the University of British Columbia in 1958 and his DDS from McGill University in 1962. He opened his dental office in Burnaby that year and continued to practise for fifty-two years, retiring at age eighty-four. He married his wife, Ina, in 1956, and together they raised their three children. This is Tom's first published work. At age ninety-three, you can still try new things and enjoy novel experiences!

DAWN COPEMAN is a writer, photographer, historian, and artist interested in all things Cumberland. Wandering the local forest trails daily, she shares her enthusiasm for slime molds, mush-rooms, lichen, and moss with anyone willing to listen. She volunteers for the Cumberland Community Forest Society and conducts tours at Coal Creek Historic Park, researching the stories of former residents and documenting the history of Cumberland Chinatown, No.1 Japanese Town, and the old mine sites for the Cumberland Museum & Archives.

RUSSELL SAKAUYE was born and raised in Toronto. Many of his cultural and culinary influences came from family gatherings and the Toronto-Japanese Canadian communities. Fond memories of bazaars, picnics, and family events inspired Russell to research and write about how food connects his family's past and present. He currently resides in Okotoks, Alberta, with his wife, son, and Winnie the family dog. In his spare time, Russell enjoys playing video games with his son, going on pottery date nights with his wife, working toward his black belt in tae kwon do, and leading the local Scouting group.

MATT RADER is the author of five books of poetry, a work of non-fiction, and the story collection *What I Want to Tell Goes Like This*, which includes several stories set in historical and contemporary Cumberland.

ANDREW FINDLAY is a freelance journalist whose work appears in a wide variety of environmental, nature, travel, outdoor, business, and lifestyle publications. He lives with his wife and two daughters in the Comox Valley, and his assignments take him around the world.

GRANT SHILLING is a writer, artist, outreach worker, and curator. He founded the nonprofit Get on Board, which uses board sports for youth outreach, and has used sport and culture as outreach with diverse populations including the Gaza Surf Club; surfing Bedouins in Alexandria, Egypt; the Rainbow Warriors street soccer team; and skateboarding youth in Ahousaht. Shilling is the author of *The Cedar Surf: An Informal History of Surfing in British Columbia* and *Surfing with the Devil: In Search of Waves and Peace in the Middle East*. He edited and published *The GIG: Gulf Islands Gazette*, a storytelling newspaper, and has had numerous gallery exhibitions. He is the proud father of Levon and has lived in Cumberland for seventeen years.

Index

Photographs and captions indicated by page numbers in italics

D

E

About the Cumberland Museum & Archives

When the last coal mine closed in 1966, visionaries of the day decided the history of Cumberland was worth preserving. Local businessman E.W. Bickle had donated the old *Comox Free Press* building at 2757 Dunsmuir Avenue to the Chamber of Commerce and by 1969 it housed the first Cumberland Museum: displays of old mining equipment, farming and household implements, items from the hospital, a few models, and a lot of photographs, staffed by retired miners and village volunteers. By 1981 the museum had outgrown the space. With village support, government grants, and fundraising efforts by the newly formed Cumberland & District Historical Society, the museum was relocated to a new building at 2680 Dunsmuir Avenue, where it is still housed today. Exhibits and programs continue to tell the stories of the people of Cumberland—the rich, the poor, the powerful, the rebellious, the righteous, and the radical.